PLANET CORONA
PETER MORTIMER
The first one hundred columns

First published 2021 by IRON Press
5 Marden Terrace
Cullercoats
North Shields
NE30 4PD
tel +44(0)191 2531901
ironpress@xlnmail.com
www.ironpress.co.uk

ISBN 978-0-9954579-8-0
Printed by Imprint Digital

© Peter Mortimer 2021

Cover and book design, Brian Grogan and Peter Mortimer

Typeset in Georgia 9pt

IRON Press books are distributed by
NBN International
and represented by Inpress Ltd
Milburn House, Dean Street
Newcastle upon Tyne NE1 1LF
tel: +44(0)191 2308104
www.inpressbooks.co.uk

Planet Corona

FOREWORD

Less than a year ago our lives were upended by a virus. Though some saw it as no worse than a spot of flu it has gone on to claim over a million lives across the world. A million and counting. Not only that, but the virulence of the thing forced us to retreat into our homes for weeks on end, splitting families and wreaking destruction on jobs and livelihoods.
Even when we ventured out again everything was different. We had to shop while wearing a mask, we couldn't stand at the bar and order a drink in a pub, schools were reorganised into "bubbles". Bubbles were just part of a new lexicon we had to grapple with, along with furloughs, lockdowns, the rule of six and the second wave. The technophobes among us had to learn quickly as we grappled with Zoom calls and the like. Our lives are ruled by apps – but are they 'appy' lives? At *The Journal* we were desperate for someone to come along and help our readers make sense of it all.

However, the only offer came from Peter Mortimer, whose instinct was to make nonsense of it all.

And now Peter has published the first 100 columns. It's a mighty effort. At one point he resolved to give up, only (like the virus) to find a second wind.

An early column consisted entirely of questions, which have scandalously yet to be addressed in any Downing Street press briefing. Another described a bus journey to an eerily deserted Newcastle city centre. And another answered a question on every Whitley Bay person's lips – whose was that old bike outside Nicholson's the butchers? And there were diversions into yoga, Brexit and the relaxing powers of a good, stiff session of ironing. It adds up to not necessarily a chronicle of our lives during the great pandemic of 2020, but an extensive footnote for historians to pore over long after our R numbers have come up. And the best of luck to them.

Richard Kirkman
Print Publishing Editor of *The Journal*

AUTHOR'S NOTE

A PERSON SLIPPING ARSE UPWARDS ON A BANANA SKIN IS THE STAPLE STUFF of farce and has often brought gales of laughter on stage or (more likely) in early films.

If that same person's fall leads to a brain haemorrhage and death, it's a different matter. Thus farce and tragedy can be close bedfellows and many things that happen in life, or in art are capable of straying into either camp. So it is with these columns. My first instinct to begin the Planet Corona column came early in lockdown. I was in the bank and walked up to the counter wearing a face mask. In normal times, this would have spread alarm. Staff never blinked an eye. This is odd, I thought, this is very odd. Something told me we were entering a whole new universe and as a writer I wanted to reflect on it, satirise it, lampoon it, weep for it, be afraid of it, question it. The incident encapsulated both the seriousness and absurdity of the situation and is mentioned in the first column published in *The Journal*. For seventy-five columns it was (Sundays apart) a daily venture. Bernard Levin did the same years back for *The Times* I recall. Miles Kington is the only other writer who to my knowledge in recent times has penned a personal daily newspaper column (most are weekly). Kington's task was more challenging, because the columns were longer, against which the whole universe was his canvas, whereas my columns gravitate round coronavirus.

Here, for your edification are the first one hundred columns which may, I hope, offer a different running perspective on this extraordinary period.

At the time of publication the column is still published twice weekly. I hope it has provided/does provide a welcome sideways look to what are often the pandemic's grim realities.

Writing it is a challenge and has often been important for me in keeping it all together in the virus's bleaker moments. In a small way, it may possibly have done the same elsewhere.

If so, jolly good. Let me thank Richard Kirkman of *The Journal* for his constant support, Eileen Jones for the careful editing and proofing, IRON Press' own Kate Jones for leading me through all the online intricacies (the columns go on my Facebook page after publication in *The Journal*) and designer Brian Grogan for his creative ideas and patience. And my partner Kitty Fitzgerald who, also being a writer, understood and dealt with the occasional tetchiness as deadlines approached with little sign of the column's completion.

And let me be the only person on earth ever to thank coronavirus for anything. A black pestilence it may be, yet its presence made possible the columns and the book. A mixed blessing in many ways, then.

Peter Mortimer
Cullercoats, November 2020.

LOWDOWN ON THE AUTHOR

PETER MORTIMER IS A MAN OF MANY PARTS, SOME OF THEM HIS OWN. He grew up in Nottingham, now lives on Tyneside and can boast a mantelpiece fairly uncluttered by literary awards. This despite decades of plays, poetry, novellas, travel books and journalism, the last pursuit with such contrasting organs as *The Guardian* and a small weekly newspaper in Walthamstow. He is regularly blown about in the windy North East coastal village of Cullercoats, where he lives. Here he runs IRON Press and Cloud Nine Theatre Productions and often talks to Cardew the Seagull (pictured) who has the good sense not to listen.

Cardew

 SATURDAY MAR 28

MY CAREER AS A BANK ROBBER AND WHY WE'RE LUCKY TO BE HERE

All doom and gloom makes Jack a dull boy and Jill a dull girl so in my daily posting I'll try and take a more offbeat look at what's happening on Planet Corona.

I live in a small Cullercoats street and found myself wondering during the pandemic about the old and the vulnerable therein, until I realised – hang on – that's you, Mortimer. I was once the new kid on the block. So just when did I become the old gadgie? Such thoughts occupy my mind as I walk into the bank. Nothing unusual in that, except when else would someone have been able to approach the counter while wearing a full face mask, without a single person blinking an eye? I was tempted to shout 'stick 'em up!' but this might be seen as bad taste.

Meantime I have signed up to become an NHS volunteer and when hearing of the half million others who have done the same, felt a surge of pride and the desire to sing a chorus of *There'll Always Be An England*.

Thank our lucky stars and stripes we are not in the USA. They have a non-existent health service and a deeply narcissistic myopic president who doesn't give a tinker's damn about anything or anyone but himself. Deaths are zooming up in the land of the free quicker than a NASA moon shot – the fastest rate on earth – but hey, the free market will sort it!

 MONDAY MARCH 30

FEAR NOT THE SHUTDOWN OF SPORT! HERE'S ONE YOU CAN TRY AT HOME

A regular correspondent, Mr. Algernon Nut, contacts me with news of a radical policy about to be introduced by the government. This takes the form of an additive to our drinking water supply and is due any day now. Called halibo, the additive – likely to prove more controversial than fluoride – ensures the impossibility of standing nearer than two metres to anyone else. This is due to to the high levels of both BO and halitosis which the additive creates in the human body. A government spokesperson conceded the move could cause a bit of a stink. Meantime with almost every sporting activity cancelled, I'm pleased to hear news of a brand new sport rapidly gaining popularity and one you can enjoy without leaving your home. The difference between Climbing the Walls and almost any other sport is with CTW the slower you can move, the better your chance of winning! Contestants are urged to post videos online to prove just how slowly they are managing to climb the walls of their living rooms. Winners will be offered priority access to the vaccine – in about one year's time.

Those with the same masochistic tendencies as myself, who listen in to *The Archers* must have become increasingly mystified how Ambridge seems the UK's only Corona-free zone (I can't speak for the telly soaps). Apparently the programme may catch up some time later this month. Can we then hope for total (and permanent) isolation of the insufferable Grundys?

TUESDAY MARCH 31

FEEL FREE TO PARTAKE OF THIS UNIQUE CORONA DIET

The Corona Diet is a little-known spin-off from the virus, but I can introduce its first success story – albeit an accidental one. Respecting social distancing, David Jamieson, the Cullercoats greengrocer, has shut the shop proper, serving his customers through a hatch. This means that for each sale, where previously he stood at the till, he is now scurrying round the shop filling bags with fruit and veg. On the move throughout the day David finds himself two stone lighter than he was in February.

We were always told fruit and veg were good for you. So it proves. David's assistant, Gillian, is equally mobile in the new set-up but was a slender lass to begin with so she has, as they say, less to lose.

It's exhausting work for both, but to the close-knit Cullercoats community, they're heroes for battling on.

The dramatic cutback globally in the activities of cars and planes and the shutdown of thousands of factories, has seen air pollution levels plummet, a blossoming of the environment, a much cleaner planet and a significant decline in environment-related deaths – deaths which have been estimated worldwide to be 400,000 a year.

Assume this number were now seen to be halved, where would it statistically leave the supposed global catastrophe of the killer virus?

And could it be that in all this mayhem, our beautiful planet is trying to tell us something important?

PLANET Corona
WED APRIL 1

SLEEPING WITH A CAT ON YOUR HEAD – DOES IT HELP?

Not too many people wearing masks, I note. I'm proud of my own (acquired by my partner Kitty). It's a class up from those flimsy affairs – ill-fitting and no defence against streetwise bugs able to slip between the gaps. These are little more than handkerchiefs with strings.

Mine is rather impressive: close-fitting, sculptured, tapering into a distinctive snout. The front bit is a special filter in blue plastic casing. I slightly resemble a *Star Wars* storm trooper and enjoy the sense of drama this can provoke in unprepared onlookers, especially if I'm also wearing my Indian hat.

I have no idea how effective the mask is, nor have all the public information bulletins had much to say on the general efficacy of masks. The mask does also make me feel rather worthy.

It does little to disguise identity hereabouts. 'Hello Pete' people say.

When all this is over, the mask will go onto one of the shop window dummies that over the years have taken residence in my house (none of whom pays a single penny in rent).

Meantime, myths have been circulating about the virus. Here's the truth. Wearing a Toon shirt gives no immunity. You cannot pick up the virus from listening to BBC Newcastle. Wearing two pairs of socks is a waste of time as a deterrent, as is shaving anti-clockwise, sleeping with a cat on your head or whistling Beethoven's Fifth on one leg. Just thought you'd like to know if you're checking online.

PLANET *Corona*
THURS APRIL 2

CHEER UP! A BREAD AND BUTTER PUDDING IS ROUND THE CORNER!

Few April Fool jokes about yesterday. I wonder why?
But pause before you sink into despair, or wring your hands, fall to your knees and wail to the heavens 'Woe is me!' In Samuel Beckett's great play *Waiting for Godot*, when told a certain activity helped pass the time, a character says 'The time would have passed anyway'. And this corona time will pass anyway. And before too long we shall look back with a sense of nostalgia. Unconvinced? Think of the devastation of World War II: the terrible loss of young lives – both on foreign fields and at home from the carnage of bombing, whole streets and communities wrecked. Think of the rationing, the black-outs, the dark days of the early 40s when all seemed lost. How grim, how sombre was the national mood.

Yet we now look back affectionately to that sense of 'the wartime spirit'. Coloured with a Vera Lynn nostalgia we come to believe they were good times when the nation pulled together with a common resolve. With the exception of a few irresponsible idiots and the ever-present criminal fraternity, we are pulling together right now: countless tales of selflessness, heroism, initiative and defiant fun, from fancy dress postmen to mass clapping, a reminder that this wretched virus will ultimately be no match for the human spirit. And this! On my doorstep, a hot bread and butter pudding cooked by my neighbour, poet Pauline Plummer. Oh, the small miracles that fortify life!

FRIDAY APRIL 3

TOTAL HYGIENE REQUIRED –
SO DON'T FORGET TO WASH THE SOAP

So Wimbledon is cancelled……. Thus, all pandemics have a silver lining. Meantime, my friend Alan Fidler, award-winning tourist guide, taxi-driver and inspiration behind the Northumbrian World War One Commemoration Project, asks this question: Why give exemption for off-licences to stay open, yet force garden centres to close?

I have no answer. And have never owned a garden. But the therapeutic benefits of pottering are undisputed (not quite so, alcohol). If you greatly reduce access to the materials that make such pottering possible, you worsen the potential mental well-being of a whole section of society.

Plus which, millions of unsaleable plants, shrubs and flowers will now simply rot away. And gardens nationwide will look bereft. A travesty. And one of the more bonkers ideas to emerge.

A word about this washing your hands business. Occasionally I become obsessive and convince myself further safeguards are needed. I devised a plan. Before using the bar of soap, you should wash it – to ensure its total hygiene. To do this, you need a second bar of soap. Though of course, this second bar may not be totally germ free and itself will need cleaning. Thus a third bar should be used to wash the second one … Hang on though – that means that – erm, well – this third bar … oh, let's just leave it.

Two choruses of *Happy Birthday* is apparently the right time span for the hand-wash. Though it is a dire tune rivalled only by *God Save the Queen* for dreariness. Alternative suggestions welcome.

SAT APRIL 4

THE LONELINESS OF THE SHORT DISTANCE COMMUTER

My writing room overlooks Cullercoats Metro and though the desk deliberately faces the wall (too easily distracted otherwise) during this pandemic I find myself swivelling round at the arrival of each train.

These are less frequent now and with far fewer passengers. Outside of the rush hour (more of a trickle hour, really) there may be only one or two people per carriage and they're well spaced out – no, not in that way.

There is something haunting about these solitary figures and how far apart they sit. For some reason, my heart goes out to them. They seem to affirm how vulnerable, how isolated and how exposed the human race can be – not a thought I'd normally harbour when watching people pop on and off a Metro ... I find these solitary travellers stay uncomfortably in my mind.

I think of the paintings of the American artist Edward Hopper. Hopper's figures are often alone, sat in an otherwise empty night-time urban bar, we, the viewer, observing from out in the street. Hopper's loners can haunt us too, can remind us of our human fragility and need to interact with others. And it's increasingly obvious the sensitivity needed when the authorities ban those same interactions long-term. Otherwise rumblings, ever louder.

I'm curious about 'furlough'. Pre-pandemic, we rarely heard the word mentioned. Many people had little clue as to its meaning. A pre-metric measurement, maybe? No, that's furlong. Now, like the virus, furlough's all over the place and no seeming antidote.

MONDAY APRIL 6

IF YOU WANT TO FEEL KARMA, WALK INTO A BIKE SHOP

Building London's Nightingale Hospital in nine days is wondrous. When my attic was built, estimated time was seven days. The builders were here six weeks, though 'here' is inaccurate as they would go missing for days on end – as builders do.

Nightingale was built by the army. I'm not sure what the army do most of the time but whenever they're called upon for other duties, I'm impressed. Why not put them in the construction trade more often? We'd soon meet our housing targets and the soldiers would be less inclined to fire off at people in foreign climes.

A puncture took me for repairs to Whiptails Bike Shop in Tynemouth. My bike is vital for sanity during this pandemic and good for social distancing. The atmosphere of a bike shop is immeasurably less hostile than a repair garage where you often collect the repaired vehicle and wait for the slow intake of breath, the shaking of the head and the news that the original estimate of £200 is now £12,745.

Whiptails is run by the affable mother and son Jill and Stuart and like all good bike shops, you know you won't be ripped off. Quite the opposite. The visit lifts my spirits and reminds me of the much-missed Lavericks in Cullercoats where I would occasionally argue that the charged repair price was too low.

Thanks to Andy Waterworth for his suggested *Happy Birthday* replacement for hand-washing – *Half Man Half Biscuit's* chorus in *Paradise Lost*. Good choice Andy.

Did you play in the Garden of Eden?/Were the goalkeeper's gloves to you tossed?/ 'Cos it seems to me you're the reason/ You're the reason why Paradise Lost.

PLANET  TUESDAY APRIL 7

THE DAFFODILS ON PLANET CORONA
ARE AS LONELY AS A CLOUD

My sympathies during this crisis lie with the daffodils. Our most ubiquitous urban flower right now, they wait yearlong for their brief Spring glory, an exuberant explosion of vibrant yellow. Such was the effect on Wordsworth he was moved to pen the immortal response 'Blimey!'

And this year? The daffodils on roadsides and traffic islands nod away almost unnoticed – lonely as a cloud while us lot are stuck indoors.

On Radio 4, some churches were arguing that cathedrals be allowed to stay open during the pandemic. Reason? They serve a deep and vital spiritual need for many people at such a time. My fictional rotund friend Geordie Porgie contacts me to say Toon fans could argue the same for St. James's Park.

This pandemic puts me in mind of the phrase of that great German thinker, Friedrich Nietzsche. 'Who talks of winning – survival is all.' Worth remembering.

Naturally I have all of Nietzsche's albums, mainly on vinyl, as is my wont. This includes the collectors' item he recorded with Dolly Parton in Cullercoats Crescent Club which includes their unforgettable version of *My Old Man's a Dustman*.

Finally, an 'umble poem penned by myself to celebrate one Corona advantage – the new mainly litter-free seafronts the 'stay-at-home' policy results in:

Farewell to the Coke cans, the Burger King muck/To the thin plastic bottles that crunch underfoot/Farewell to crisp packets, empty cartons of fags/To the tossed away wrappings, the remains of kebabs/The fish and chip boxes you just hoy on the floor/How lovely without them. Could you do it no more?

SARTRE'S HELL AND THOSE VORACIOUS SEAGULLS

Apologies for this column's non-appearance yesterday. Circumstances, as they say, beyond my control.

The virus sees three humans, one dog and various shop window dummies holed up in this Cullercoats house. When all other distractions fail, we can wave at the infrequent passing Metros or talk to slugs.

As with the entire planet now, it's not always easy. My partner Kitty suffered two slipped discs before the lockdown. The excellent chiropractor she found locally is now closed, so no treatment. Wakanda, who hails from The Republic of the Congo woke up a few days ago with a bad back pain which left him moving awkwardly. Sleeping on a hard floor has improved matters, though not ideal for untroubled slumber. Neither indulges the 'poor me' syndrome – invariably self-defeating. They concentrate on the positives, which hereabouts are many. The sea is round the corner, three is better than one, the sun shines and there are four jars of Sue Pethybridge's home-made marmalade...

Three is the number in Jean Paul Sartre's play *Huis Clos* (In Camera). That particular trio's incarceration was eternal – they were dead. The play's famous phrase is 'Hell is other people', though it can be the lack of other people too. Ask those alone in a 20 storey tower block.

Another French language writer, the late Albert Camus (who incidentally played in goal for Algeria) is seeing a revival of his pertinent novel *The Plague*. Well worth a read, if hardly a rib-tickler. Caroline Fox gets in touch re my poem on the refreshing lack of litter on the seafront. 'You fail to touch upon the plight of the seagulls who no longer have Greggs/fish and chip shop scraps to feast upon and look thoroughly hacked off,' says Caroline. Fair dos.

 FRIDAY APRIL 10

I CAN SEE CLEARLY NOW THE BEER HAS GONE

Reasons you might prefer to be this side of the Atlantic right now: (No.4) since the outbreak two millions guns have been sold in the USA, and gun stores – officially classed as essential outlets – are allowed to stay open.

And if that doesn't frighten the virus, nothing will.

My vote for the current least desirable job? Advertising director for the Mexican beer company, Corona. Though I checked them out and discovered since the outbreak they've given up the ghost and ceased production; the job no longer exists.

Cycling along the seafront I marvelled at the pinprick clarity of Tynemouth Priory, one of life's great vistas. It's one benefit of the lockdown; the clean unpolluted air which sharpens all aspects of land and seascapes … How ironic that this cleaner air is also the carrier of the deadly virus that does battle with our species.

 SATURDAY APRIL 11

NEVER MIND THE CATASTROPHE, WHAT ABOUT GEORGE ALAGIAH'S WALLPAPER?

I like the way some things are being turned back to front now. Thus we normally welcome newscasters and other TV reporters into our homes via the small (or these days often monstrous) screen but now we are also being invited into theirs.

Increasingly, corona restrictions mean some news items and even the weather are being beamed direct not from the studio but from the reporter's own living room or kitchen.

Even previously, I often felt guilty when a newscaster was announcing some mass murder or other cataclysmic event to find myself thinking, 'hmm, I'm sure she's had those roots touched' or maybe, 'that tie with that shirt? I don't think so,' by which time the item is finished and I've no idea of the subject matter. This is one advantage of news on the radio.

Now there are other visual distractions. Musing on the choice of

Kathy Clugston's scatter cushions or wondering just why George Alagiah chose that awful wallpaper or why Robert Peston hasn't washed out the cafetiere, has brought an entire new element to watching the news.

I ponder the potential dangers of these new domestic relocations. What if the newscaster's partner, momentarily forgetting the new discipline, walks into camera bringing a cup of tea and a digestive biscuit?

Or we hear shouts from the other room, 'Well, are you taking this dog out or not!' A jam covered child may suddenly enter stage left and start climbing all over Fiona Bruce. It would add to the fun and fun is what we need right now.

MONDAY APRIL 13

THE VITAL QUESTION – WHY DO PAINT POT LIDS NEVER FIT?

One unremarked symptom of the stay-at-home dynasty is how it can slowly turn you into a sartorial slob.

The risk is you roll out of bed, shower, pull on a pair of tracky bottoms and a t-shirt then mooch around the house. Not going out can weaken the instinct to look your best.

Though when such torpor descends, doing something practical can work wonders. I totally surprised myself by taking a deep breath, then trimming the hedge, taking a strimmer to the tiny lawn, and painting a garden chair. All this, from a horticultural pygmy. And straight after, I put on my best duds and danced around the house.

One question though: why do tins of paint have lids which are (a) almost impossible to open and (b) almost impossible to close – and it has always been the same. There's a fortune to be made for some innovator.

My favourite word right now is Covidiots. This describes those who deliberately ignore advice on measures which might best help contain the virus.

To cheer you up, let me point out that the environmental effect of the shut-downs thus far is the equivalent of every vehicle in the country being electrically powered. Can we somehow not lose these new benefits when normality returns? Thanks.

I later engaged in the totally useless pursuit of how many anagrams I could make from the words 'corona' and 'covid', separately or together. But the duo are stubbornly resistant in more ways than one.

Not a single anagram – why not try it yourself?

PLANET Corona TUESDAY APRIL 14

AN AUDIENCE OF MINUS TWO – THE PULLING POWER OF POETRY

One can only feel for those megastars, normally used to an audience of thousands or tens of thousands, doing their stuff in front of a handful of technicians or officials. How unloved must they feel! These 'ghost' performances could be in a theatre, an opera house, St Peter's Square (under which sign I once saw scrawled So is The Pope!) or an open arena.

For some of us, such numbers are nothing strange.

As a poet of minimal output and even more minimal reputation, very occasionally (and let's not put it any higher) I am asked to give a reading. Early fantasies of a Glastonbury-style surge for tickets were slowly replaced by a quiet satisfaction if the audience exceeded ten. For the launch of one poetry book not a single person turned up.

This was a record I thought hard to beat until the tireless poet and broadcaster Ian McMillan informed me otherwise. He once read to an audience of minus two. The first half was an 'open mic' session. Present were Ian and two audience members who both read their own work before the interval. The two then went home.

Boris Johnson has had some sort of epiphany post-Covid, physically and otherwise. The man is barely recognisable from the smirking patrician who once saw politics as a jape and us as his playthings.

What other Tory leader would utter words such as these?

'We will defeat this virus. We will defeat it with love'. Ian Duncan Smith anyone? Margaret Thatcher?

We can only hope the metamorphosis is not fleeting.

PLANET Corona
WEDNESDAY APRIL 15

MORTIMER'S NEW RANGE OF DENTISTS' HARDWARE FOR THE CORONA AGE

The pandemic emphasises the vital role played by NHS staff, bus drivers, refuse collectors, social workers, supermarket employees, care home staff, postal delivery people et al. What unites them all? They get paid peanuts.

We couldn't do without these people. The system would collapse. Many put their own lives at risk every day.

Meantime there is a whole slew of people at the top of the tree and if they didn't turn up for work for a few days, we'd probably not notice the difference. The second group of people get paid often twenty times as much as the first group of people.

Funny, isn't it?

Controversy rages about the efficiency of face masks. Are they any use for the general public? Might we just as well wear a cream cake on our head? The experts seem divided.

Who are we to believe? My current face mask is black and I wear it with a royal blue bandana whenever I'm out. I tell myself this is the action of a responsible citizen keen to do his bit. Secretly, I quite like emerging from the house looking like a masked avenger.

To prevent the rise in dental decay and toothache and confront the problem (given social distancing requirements) of unemployed dentists, I offer three new products. The Mortimer Probe, Drill and Needle can now be purchased at reasonable price. Each is two metres long. Only one person came up with a successful anagram combining the words corona and covid. Step forward Eileen Jones with her phrase 'raccoon void' – an absence of stripy tailed bandits. A packet of chocolate digestives is on its way.

THURSDAY APRIL 16

BLAME IT ALL ON THE EVIL DR MALEFACORUM FROM NORTH BLYTH

Virus theories abound! I treat with caution the online claim that raspberry ripple works as an antidote. It is effective apparently only if eaten at an exact time of the day, dependent on your date of birth. Forward that DOB information to a post box number to get your own details – oh yes, plus £500. This includes the price of the ripple.

Theory two has the virus arriving in a small, undetectable space craft, despatched from the dying planet Dunk, whose inhabitants will populate Earth once corona has wiped us out. Conventional combat is difficult as Dunkians are only one millimetre tall and quite flabby. Anyway, there are only five of them.

Or you can blame the Chinese because they don't like the Americans, or blame the Americans because they don't like the Chinese, or blame President Putin because he doesn't like either of them, or blame Mrs Putin because she doesn't like her husband. One theory says the virus was released by the disgruntled Man City Supporters Club, desperate to stop Liverpool clinching the title. Another, a rejected contestant from *Love Island*.

Could it be the fault of Jacob Rees-Mogg who for his sins has been incarcerated in the cellar of a gloomy Scottish castle? Well – has anyone seen him?

Or that there is no virus at all and we are subject to a global mass hypnosis by the evil yet omnipotent Doctor Malefacorum, from North Blyth.

Or you can blame me if you like because I remember failing to wash my hands after scratching my nose on Feb 27th.

Mea culpa!

PLANET    FRIDAY APRIL 17

CONGRATULATIONS! YOU QUALIFY FOR PREFERENTIAL TREATMENT!

(NOW READ ON.....)

A call comes through from my local Health Centre.

'And how are we today, Mr. Mortimer?'

'We? Well, I'm OK. Not sure about you.'

'Just a routine check. Are you displaying any symptoms?'

'Symptoms? An itchy ear, but no, not really.'

'You could qualify for preferential treatment.'

'Preferential treatment?'

'Those of a certain age – you are of a certain age, aren't you?'

'I certainly am.'

'We could express you onto a corona ward.'

'Express me? Onto a corona ward?'

'Immediately. A precaution. Then you may be eligible for our "Spoilt For Choice" scheme.'

'What is that?'

'It's an exclusive ward. Where you can relax. No worries about the huge stress the responsibility of a future choice may put you under. You sign the document, no more worries.'

'What choice? What document?'

'The big choice. One you shouldn't need to face alone. We are here for you.'

'And the document?'

'The document giving us permission not to resuscitate if we felt it necessary.'

'Resuscitate? But I'm not ill.'

'Call it preventive medicine.'

'You want me to let you knock me off whenever you feel like it?'

'Not resuscitate. Only if we felt it necessary.'

'Not resuscitate? That could just mean you do me in when I'm asleep!'

'Please think about it.'

'I get it. The government haven't got enough equipment and

protective clothing to go round and to cover up have worked out how to get rid of the most expendable people.'
'Only when we feel it necessary. We'll check again tomorrow. Meantime, stay home, protect the NHS, save lives. Goodbye.'

PLANET Corona
SATURDAY APRIL 18

AND NOW THE SPORTS NEWS...
HANG ON? WHAT SPORT?

At times like these my heart goes out to those stalwarts of journalism, the sports reporters. Imagine a chef with no ingredients, a magician with no conjuring tricks, an astronaut without a space craft, a– (OK, enough of that – Ed.)

What we have now is sports reporters without sport. When I was a film and theatre critic my weekly output depended to a great degree on watching films, going to plays. This seemed a sine qua non of the job.

Yet somehow, every day, every newspaper in a world without sport still has several sporting pages. A miracle? A sleight of hand? A brilliant illusion?

When our creative artists set to bringing forth the corona fiction, theatre and film, what better subject matter for a work of absurdity? I might even write it myself.

Already I imagine the editor, stomping round the newsroom in a state of apoplexy, stabbing his finger at the hapless sports reporters.

'I don't care if there is no sport! You just get out there and write about it anyway!'

Because Marx was wrong. Religion is no longer the opium of the people. Sport is.

Ever wondered what the word covid means? The Oxford English Dictionary has it thus; 'A lineal measure formerly used in India. It varied from 36 inches to 14 inches.' None the wiser, I went online. It's from the virus family name apparently, CoV. Not that exciting. Oh, yes, the next time you have a wash in the sink, check the water before you pull the plug. At least 50 per cent cleaner. Small silver lining...

 MONDAY APRIL 20

HOW TO SUCK SOUP THROUGH A MASK.........

A Mrs Drain, from the People's Republic of West Boldon, enquires when and where should we be wearing masks. Nobody seems certain. A few hints below:

IN THE SHOWER

Not recommended. It seriously affects the quality of the singing, the audibility of the vocals and most people who do it, can't sing anyway.

DURING SEX

This is optional, but not recommended for those who enjoy verbal communication during the process. Masks do offer kinky possibilities but this is not the publication to consider these. Nor are masks recommended for casual sex. In such dangerous times only dumbos would go down that road anyway.

WHEN EATING

Practical problems. Soup is possible, as liquid fodder could be sucked through the mask filter. The minestrone soup served lunchtimes in some Italian restaurants is so thin that it may be the best choice, offering at least some solids ... Somewhat messy though ...

Lockdown offers new reading opportunities, yet somehow, as a slow reader, I am still on the same novel I was on when all this began. In my defence, it is a long one. Writing fares little better. The new opportunities have mainly been wasted. My fellow Nottingham-born author here, Steve Chambers, tells me he has written more than 10,000 words of a new novel since start of lockdown. I seethe inwardly.

Compensation? On quick calculation, this column for the last three weeks tots up to more than 5,000 words. 'Serious' writers are often snobbish about journalism, just as journalists see being called 'too literary' an insult. Best just to write, leave definitions to others.

TUESDAY APRIL 21

THE MIRACLE OF BUSES AND THE WONDER OF HAIKU

During the pandemic I am increasingly staring at buses. There is something terribly lonely about buses now. They are ghost ships adrift on the ocean. Invariably they are empty or virtually empty – strange enough in daylight. But to see an empty bus emerging from the darkness, fierce white light shimmering from every window, is like some sci-fi or supernatural apparition.

In normal times, using to the full my pass, I would often jump on a bus for no reason at all. The No.1 to Kibblesworth became my favourite, a journey into, through, then out of Newcastle. Spend some time following your own unplanned inclinations in the old pit village (it has a pub and a CIU club) then the return journey. Sitting on the upstairs front seat offered a unique form of travel, a lofty wobbly panorama of urban life below, a sneaky peek into yards and gardens otherwise shielded by high walls. At that height you are king of the road.

Now, such journeys are rightly discouraged. Yet drivers still trundle their buses from A to B, passing one deserted stop after another, sucking their cough sweet or whistling to retain morale. Some drivers, the miserabilists who normally scowl silently at every boarding passenger, may welcome this. The majority ache like the rest of us; that terrible lack of human contact, that painful isolation.

Meantime, some comfort in the way haiku writers distil life's too often overlooked small details, quiet moments seeing things anew. Try this one, then read a lot more;

In a bookstore/two flies settle/on a romance (Jackie Hardy).

 PLANET Corona

WEDNESDAY APRIL 22

LOCKDOWN MEANS NOT WORRYING ABOUT WHAT YOU MIGHT BE MISSING

For the first time, those morally bankrupt car adverts can lay claim to a sliver of truth. For years the ads have shown gleaming new models, either in town centres or spectacular countryside, travelling along empty, silent roads.

Car reality is more usually choking, congested streets or highways. Yet bliss! Corona has forced most of those polluting beasts back in the garage or driveway; for once, empty roads are more than an adman's fantasy and the ads are almost accurate. Oh that it could last!

The most bonkers decision was to close council tips on the argument social distancing was impossible. How come supermarkets can each day successfully sell thousands of different products to thousands of customers and a tip can't organise considerably fewer folk to turn up and dump their unloved outcasts?

And so, ugly and illegal roadside dumps of rubbish, mattresses, clapped-out freezers, cookers and microwaves become ever more frequent sights in our beautiful countryside and our throw-away society moves to a new level.

The current almost universal lack of social engagements isn't all bad. I have spent much of my life worrying I might be missing something, at parties moving constantly from one room to another, fearful the action may be elsewhere. Often I try to cram in three things in a time span suitable for one. Ridiculous, says my partner Kitty and she's right.

But now, for a time, I can relax.

No-one is going out and having fun. We're all locked down in our own homes. I can feel reassured. I'm not missing much at all.

FRIDAY APRIL 24

THE UNSEEN SCANDAL – THANK YOU CORONAVIRUS FOR EXPOSING IT

Apologies for the column's non-appearance yesterday. Reasons unknown (it was written as normal). Onwards.

Even at the best of times (and these are not they) St. George's Day passes almost unnoticed. The date was yesterday. See what I mean? As this was also the date Shakespeare was born and also the date Shakespeare died, a few moments of dancing in the street (keeping socially distant of course) might have been in order and boosted national morale.

What would the Bard have made of the current crisis? *A plague on both your houses* maybe *(Romeo & Juliet)*? Not much help. Maybe this reassurance that all things eventually pass? *Come what come may, time and the hour runs through the roughest day (Macbeth)*.

Meantime, little surprise here at the corona care homes scandal. Care homes have been a national disgrace for years, underfunded, understaffed, places where society can shut away and conveniently forget the old and the feeble. We invest little money and no imagination in these places, plonking the residents day after day around the perimeter of a soulless room, to stare at the endless blaring inanities of daytime television in which few of them are interested.

Why don't the residents have computers? Pets? Visiting children? Why don't they have a bar for pre-meal drinks? I experienced several care homes during my own parents' and other people's declining years. Each visit left me deeply depressed. Small wonder the pandemic is running riot there. These residents are sitting targets.

As more TV items in the pandemic are beamed direct from reporters' homes, (which produces technical problems) 'out of sync' sound becomes ever more common. And the new game is, which will finish first, the voice or the mouth? Place your bets.

PLANET

SAT APRIL 25

ONLY IN THIS COLUMN! THE ANSWERS TO ALL THE QUESTIONS YOU ASK!

Exclusive news via your correspondent's tireless research of Pres.Trump's latest tactics to beat corona.

Firstly: concentrated bleach injected directly into the eyeball which will catch the virus unawares.'Nobody likes bleach,' said Trump. 'Especially this turkey. Die, enemy!'

Secondly: a small rat (on a lead) fed into the rectum then tugged out after 15 mins. As the president says, no rat has caught the virus and is therefore the perfect weapon to (quote) 'scratch that mother of a virus's eyes out'.

Thirdly: ensure everyone spend a short spell inside a blast furnace. Again, to quote: 'The virus don't like heat. See how the dude tackles 500 degrees. Gone. Finished. End of.'

Meantime more tireless research this side of the pond has unearthed a confidential document about to be sent to all ministers. The document gives guidance on how they should answer leading queries thereby avoiding future confusion and obfuscation.

SHOULD WE BE WEARING MASKS?

Answer: yes but there again no, possibly, maybe.

HOW LONG WILL THE LOCKDOWN LAST?

Four weeks, or thirteen weeks, or till next year, or later, or the end of time, or all of the above.

EXACTLY WHEN CAN WE GO OUT?

For exercise. Maybe to clap on the doorstep? Deliver food to starving octogenarians? Dig the allotment. Maybe never? Or something else.

WHAT IS THE PERIOD OF SELF ISOLATION IF WE SHOW SYMPTOMS?

Seven days, or it could be fourteen days, depending. Or 28 days.

WHEN WILL SOCIAL DISTANCING BE RELAXED?

In the future. Not the past. Definitely in the future.

All the above are intended to counter criticism that we, the public, are being kept in the dark.

MONDAY APRIL 27

'YET NOW THE DAYS ROLL OUT FLAT AND FEATURELESS'

How strange to live in a time when the days have no familiar shape. On Planet Corona each day is little different to any other. Where is that Friday anticipation of the approaching weekend, the Saturday sense of a nation strolling stress free through its leisure time? Where are the Sundays, still with a leisure atmosphere but tinged with the slight deflatory feel of next week's work looming? Gone.

Many, who silently whooped with delight at the unexpected casting off of work's shackles now yearn for the companionship, the tittle-tattle, the vital trivia it embraced.

Writers are said to be used to solitude and thereby cope better. Not this one. Once away from the writing desk, I ache for social interaction.

Yet now the days roll out flat and featureless. I flick through my diary, pages either empty or with crossed-out events and meetings, doomed now never to happen.

Throughout the planet, millions of people face similar social damage as this tiny germ devastates fabrics of entire societies. And though I am not religious, my pantheistic tendencies come to the fore. Pantheism denies the existence of an individual god; the universe itself is the power. Its more fashionable contemporary shape is in James Lovelock's Gaia theory.

Corona has created this anomaly – our production and consumption is battered, but with a huge improvement to the environment. Is the virus warning us we can never go back; that post-Corona, we must live life more simply, less voraciously? If so, should we ironically look again at Corona, not as our destroyer, but our potential saviour?

TUESDAY APRIL 28

'CLAPPING IS FOR THE LIVING. THE DEAD DESERVE SILENCE'

A word about clapping, which many of us now indulge each Thursday at 8pm. I have no idea why we strike our hands together to express appreciation or gratitude, but we do. Sometimes this is abused. At a few football grounds, when honouring the death of some notable, the authorities dropped the minute silence in favour of clapping. This was a safety measure. Too many yobbos were sabotaging the silence, by shouts, whistles etc; hard to sabotage 40,000 people clapping. Though the change diluted the sense of dignity and respect afforded by the ritual. Clapping is for the living. The dead deserve silence.

In some political regimes (the more autocratic) clapping can be a stressful business. You don't want to be the first to stop applauding your great leader's conference speech. Such things are noted and could lead to a lifetime of rock-breaking. Reports of some party stooges – sorry loyal supporters – continuing to clap long after the conference has ended are surely exaggerated as is the one of the delegate still clapping the great leader when he dropped dead (the delegate not the leader) though whether through exhaustion or starvation was not recorded.

The Thursday clapping is for the NHS but it is also for ourselves. The communal activity releases something in us. At a time of isolation we are being seen to do our bit, not alone but together. We are bonded with our neighbours, despite that recent slanging match over next-door's dog pooing on your lawn or you never having exchanged a single word with No.26 in ten years. Regardless, clap on!

THE RITUALISTIC WEEKLY HUNTING
OF THE BINS – GREAT FUN!

Probably the most succinct quote on the fate of the human race – eleven words with a curious relevance to our coronavirus capers – came from Robert Newman at the end of his splendid Radio 4 programme, *The Extinction Tapes*.
'Those societies on the wrong side of nature have no future.'
He's got it in one. But are we all listening?
The pandemic has produced a range of previously unsung heroes, from bus and delivery drivers, supermarket workers, NHS staff or course, but the last week has thrown up a new species – refuse collectors.
Someone's splendid idea was to stick a message to the wheelie bins thanking the collectors for maintaining their service in such difficult times. I immediately did the same, mainly in genuine thanks but also, I confess a secret hope it may curry favour with them when I put outside the gate some awkward future item.
We know our bin men (why no women?) mainly by their back lane shouts and the whirring sounds of bins being ceremoniously hoisted onto the rear of the wagon to give up their sacrificial offering into the grinding jaws of the Beast.
Also ritualistic is their replacing of the bins, it being a rule that no bins should be put back outside their own gate, but generously scattered along the length of the lane.
The habit has led to a new sport of bin-hunting, the sight of neighbours wandering the length of the lane in the search for their own bin.
This is eventually located with a small sense of relief, a mini-version of that sensation of finally finding your lost child in the crowd.

PLANET Corona

THURSDAY APRIL 30

'FEW PEOPLE ARE A QUARTER OF A CENTURY OLDER THAN ME'

Had anyone forecast a few months ago that a news story would appear whose coverage would dwarf the two year daily Brexit exposure, we would have locked them up. Yet here's Corona. A quick count of the news stories (excluding sport) in yesterday's copy of *The Journal* revealed 33 – 28 of them Corona related. Beat that, Brexit!

I find myself thinking about Captain Marvel – otherwise known as Tom Moore. Few people are a quarter century older than me (how heartening!). It's also the humble and uncynical incorruptibility of the man.

He was hoping to raise £100 from his epic walking 100 lengths of his garden on his zimmer frame; I suspect he would have felt satisfied simply to achieve his target. The amount has risen now by 280,000 per cent to £28m – 280,000 per cent! That's a bigger hike than the ever-increasing budget for the building of HSR2! (Whatever happened to that story?)

Yet the razzmatazz seems not to have phased the Captain one jot. As far as I know, he has appeared on no TV chat show. May he resist any invite to join the likes of *Celebrity Big Brother*. He is that rare commodity, a celebrity seemingly without ego (some celebs' egos are so huge they need a wing built on their gated home to accommodate it).

The Captain's version of *You'll Never Walk Alone* has also made No.1 in the charts. Though understandably at age 99 and seven eighths, Tom's vocal skills do not rival Pavarotti's, a fact which matters to none of us.

PLANET *Corona*

FRIDAY MAY 1

AN OPEN LETTER TO THE PRIME MINISTER

Dear Boris Johnson,

Well, it's been quite a month for you. First, close to death with Covid 19, then very close to a birth – that of your new son. My brother Alex thinks that given your classical background and your own recent experience, you should call the lad Ovid. He was the Latin poet who died 2000 years ago and who's always misquoted. What Ovid actually said was, 'fortune and love favour the brave'.

Time for you to be brave.

Just over a month ago you asked us, the British public, to make the greatest lifestyle sacrifices we've ever known. Virtually overnight we gave up almost all social, cultural and sporting activities. Gone for many was work (and often wages) meeting friends and relatives, gone were pubs, cafés and restaurants, gone were most shops, gone was any social grouping, travel on public transport, theatres, cinemas, concerts.

Gone were parties, foreign holidays, friends, libraries, day trips to the countryside. Gone was most semblance of the normal life we had once lived.

But we did it. We locked ourselves away. Because we understood. The odd loony apart, we showed ourselves to be a mature and responsible democracy. I was proud of us all.

I still am. But now I feel we're being short-changed, patted on the head, patronised, treated like children.

We know this pandemic is far from over. Just as our sacrifices are far from over. But we are being told not to make a fuss, that you know best and you may just reveal to us at some indefinite time in the future the timetable for the first teeny steps of an exit plan, but not now, not now.

This isn't good enough. Other advanced democracies (I discount the Land of the Orange Lunatic) are now keeping their populations informed on future plans, however preliminary and tentative those plans may be.

You are not. And you risk losing the goodwill of the British

people if you continue in this vein. Lose that goodwill and we have lost the battle.
Then it's RIP all of us.
Think carefully. Take us on board.
Best wishes, yrs etc ...

PLANET *Corona*

SATURDAY MAY 2

WELCOME TO THE CITY CROWDED ONLY IN MEMORY

Only Essential Travel reads the sign but I want to write about the city centre mid-pandemic – and that's essential. My first time on a Metro in a month.
As many checkies as passengers. Yet social distancing dictates no checking. More checkies at Haymarket but passengers straight through the open barriers unchecked. Life has become absurd.
At Haymarket there's a small street-cleaning wagon, its whirring brushes desperate to suck up litter – but there is none to suck up.
Northumberland Street – I sit eating a pasty from Milligans and attract the biggest crowd of the day – ten pigeons fighting over the occasional lobbed morsel.
Most shops closed, M&S open (curiously) also Sainsbury's Local, Superdrug and the shop no-one likes, W.H.Smith. Arch-villain Ashley's Sports Direct closed.
Only one rough sleeper. Strangely he's on his feet, chatting to three coppers pleased to have something to do.
At Grey's Monument his Earlship looks down on an almost empty Grey Street whose Georgian curves are 'unrivalled anywhere', wrote poet John Betjeman.
Shattering the eerie quiet – the pipe layers' pneumatic drills outside Pret A Manger. No buskers. Grainger Market just about open, its one entrance guarded by two functionaries. 'Which stall are you after?' they ask. I slink off.
High Friars Lane, alongside Tyneside Cinema, normally al fresco coffee and cakes the year round for Tyneside hipsters. Not a table, person or double shot latte in view. The Laing Gallery

poster advertises a never to be seen exhibition – William and Evelyn De Morgan (March-June). How sad.
No pubs, cafés, restaurants, galleries, cinemas and – leading question – where on earth can I pee?

PLANET Corona
MONDAY MAY 4

THE GOOD NEWS! I GET THE MAXIMUM DISCOUNT POSSIBLE!

I decided on a seafront stroll and checked the seagulls were socially distancing. Not entirely. Cavorting is more the word. A man sat on the next bench and seemed to be studying me. He spoke.
'Apparently', he said, 'you stand twice as much chance of getting the virus, if you are male. You are male, aren't you?'
'It's one of life's few certainties', I replied.
'Hmmmm.'
A few seconds, then he spoke again.
'Apparently,' he said, 'over 75, chances of getting the virus increase considerably. Are you over 75?'
'It's a close-run thing,' I said, 'but yes.'
'Hmmmm.'
Another pause.
'Apparently', he said, 'in a deprived region chances of dying of the virus are double that of in an affluent region. Live in the North East, do you?'
'J'y suis, j'y reste,' I answered pretentiously, though Napoleon said it first.
'Hmmmm. One of the poorest parts of the country, the North East,' he said.
A short silence, then he spoke again.
'Got any coughing?'
'Sorry, right out of coughing.'
'Do you have a temperature?'
'I certainly do have, 38 degrees.'
'Short of breath?'
'No, but I'm running short of toilet rolls.'

'Hmmmm. Have you made any arrangements?'
'Arrangements?'
He passed me his card. It read *Mr. Hip Hip Hooray Funeral Director Dead Good.*
'You get a priority discount,' he said. 'Five per cent for each negative.'
'Negative?'
'Age, sex, location. Fifteen per cent discount in all. Don't delay.'
'Actually,' I said, 'I wouldn't mind delaying a bit.'
He stood up and doffed his hat.
'Your good health.'
And at that, Mr Hip Hip Hooray took his leave while the seagulls cavorted on.

TUESDAY MAY 5

THE NOSTALGIA OF JUST SIX WEEKS AGO

Nostalgia is more rife in this region than most – occasionally to debilitating levels.

Maybe it's because of the rough justice historically suffered that as an antidote, we like nothing more than what I call 'sepiarising' the past. I say 'we', though I grew up in Nottingham with only a half century of residence here to support my use of that word. We reminisce on those good old days when we would dance happily in the back lane with rickets, or sing as we wiped our bottoms with torn off sheets of newspaper in the freezing back yard netty.

What has all this to do with Corona? Only that the virus has brought nostalgia to a new level.

Recently, I found myself with nose pressed to the window of the Rockliffe Arms in Whitley Bay, like some poor waif in a Victorian melodrama sent to bring home his drunken father.

Clustered round the empty tables inside I could see the ghosts of my friends and loved ones. They were laughing merrily, bonhomie and humour were flowing like honey. Ah, sweet memory! I was almost sick with nostalgia and not for some long gone decade but for six weeks previously. Fewer than fifty days

in the past and already I had mythologised it.
Is this a good or a bad thing? Any thoughts to the email below please. As a side-note, for those who want a vividly objective and comprehensive view of our region and its history, Dan Jackson's recent brilliant book *The Northumbrians* is a must – his obvious love of his native North East undistorted by soft indulgence or sentimentality.

PLANET *Corona*   WEDNESDAY MAY 6

THE BREATH OF FRESH AIR THAT IS JACINDA ARDEN

A small thought: the two nations most likely to come out one and two in corona deaths are the USA and the UK. These two have been the main proponents in western democracies of the free market economy and a shrinking of the state (which of course here includes the NHS). It may all be coincidental.

Meantime, Alan Fidler reminds me that North Tyneside (my own hunting ground) has one of the lowest corona rates in the country, with the coast itself doing particularly well.

I'm not surprised. Few germs can pass easily between people when they're no sooner breathed out than whisked off to harmlessness over the North Sea in the prevailing westerlies force six. Our famous winds do have compensations.

Three observations on politicians' most common platitudes during all this and what those platitudes really mean.

'You know as well as I do' - I am about to introduce a previously unknown and unprovable fact.

'I would be the last to claim everything is perfect, but –' this is my technique in answering justifiable criticism that something has become a total shambles.

'Well, I don't know about the deaths in care homes, but what I do know is –' my shameless attempt to stonewall any pertinent and potentially damaging question by changing the subject entirely.

These thoughts come to mind when watching the New Zealand prime minister Jacinda Ardern (still only 39) the world's youngest ever female head of state. She seems refreshingly free of obfuscation and verbal padding and after listening to her non-opaque thoughts on various matters, I feel fortified and enlivened. Few politicians can do that.

PLANET Corona
THURSDAY MAY 7

'COLD MUDDY PITCHES, FREEZING CHANGING ROOMS, NO SHOWERS'

And thus the world polarises into separate camps. Camp one are slowly going mad. They have already eaten the budgie, unpicked the carpet, boiled their socks, stared hard at a crumb on the kitchen table, bellowed in a dark room, watched the same box set thirty times. Occasionally they yell 'Help!' through the letterbox to an audience of none.

Camp two are totally relaxed. Each morning they rise slowly, recline with a good book, coffee and croissants. They potter about the garden and recall how they have cast off that routine of crawling from bed at 6.15am, cramming packed tight into a Metro for the twice daily commute to a meaningless job. Plus a pig of a boss, the halitosis of the person at the next desk and the prospect of another fifteen years before retirement.

Now they've discovered cloud-staring, imagining animals, faces, the shape of trees.

Meantime some premier league footballers are complaining they may be asked to play matches in empty stadiums. Where is the motivation of a passionate crowd they ask, where is the excitement, the adrenalin? What, they ask, driving off in their Maserati, is the point?

And I recall my many years of amateur football, cold muddy pitches, freezing changing rooms, no showers, kit-washing, an occasional audience of one, paying weekly subs, putting up nets, organising transport, fund-raising.

Get a life, you pros. Remember, we play football for the love of the game, for our enjoyment. Everything else, lifestyle, loot, packed stadiums, adoration, is a bonus, a privilege. If you lose temporarily one of those privileges, tough. You'll survive.

FRIDAY MAY 8

'THE RESULTING GURGLES AND CHORTLINGS LIFTED MY SPIRITS'

And lo, the son did receive from the father thirty ducats a week which were but poor offerings so he did ask of the father, that this could be one hundred ducats a week and the father said, yeah, by the month's end it will be so.

And by the month's end it was so and the son was pleased. But lo, came the next week and the father did give the son only eighty ducats and the son did complain. Did I not promise one hundred ducats at the month's end, spake the father and did I not do as I promised? And the son was sad his father had chosen to deceive him, which was a bad thing.

Meantime, King Lear says *When we are born we cry that we are come to this great stage of fools*, which is true enough but it's not long before babies are laughing too.

Radio 4's *Woman's Hour* – which even before feminism was fashionable was a pioneering, passionate, entertaining voice – asked listeners to send recordings of their babies laughing.

This is a brilliantly simple idea. The resulting gurglings, guffaws and cherubic chortlings lifted my spirits as much as anything during the pandemic.

Laughter is not always like this; as we get sullied by experience, it can become cynical, sardonic, too knowing, even cruel. There is a theory that babies are born knowing everything and slowly unlearn it as they journey through life.

They certainly know how to laugh, an expression of pure, undiluted joy. Let it wash all over us as much and often as possible.

PLANET Corona

SATURDAY MAY 9

'SUCH A DEVOTEE, HE BRINGS HIS SECATEURS TO CLEAR THE ROUTE'

My curiosity on how dental patients were faring in the pandemic is partly satisfied with news that some are pulling their own teeth.

In the old cartoon comics, the unfortunate sufferer, a bandage wrapped vertically round the head and knotted at the top, would tie a string to the tooth, the other end attached to an open door which was then slammed shut.

My own recommendation, that dentists should be supplied with two metre long drills, probes and needles (this column April 15) has been ignored.

The two following statements, both issued by leading medical officials can obviously be reconciled, but at first glance seem contradictory.

Firstly: you have a much greater chance catching the virus indoors than outdoors.

Secondly: stay indoors.

We were being asked to celebrate VE day but the whole thing felt surreal. I somehow couldn't bring myself to stick up bunting (my house exterior is colourfully decorated as it is).

And a mass chorus of *We'll Meet Again*, given that we are praying the virus will go away forever, might just be tempting fate.

A ten mile bike ride round the borough's waggonways brought an afternoon of arboreal idyll, a secluded and peaceful world only spitting distance (sorry!) from built-up urbanity. Fellow cyclist and our guide Alan Fidler led myself and The Irishman Tommy McClements round the leafy and peaceful splendours of this unique facility. Fidler informs me North Tyneside is blessed with 100 miles of the same. He is such a devotee he brings along his secateurs to clear the overgrown bits. Alan Shearer. Wonderful.

I only partially spoiled the party by falling off my bike.

PLANET

MONDAY MAY 11

THE REDUNDANT DIARY AND THE STIRRINGS OF HORTICULTURE

I open my diary. Normally it would be crammed with dates of the world book tour, meeting the agent to sign the latest film rights, a flight to the National Theatre to discuss the new play, then – (this wild fantasising has to stop – Ed).

OK. But the diary, like many people's is now as empty as a desert. One scribbled daily note reads 'Write Column.'

Will do.

As if not bad enough that our leading football team is to be sold to gangsters and we are the worst affected area for Covid 19, we are also suffering the coldest weather.

Elsewhere people loll about in the mid twenties. Here the bitter east winds off the North Sea mean that despite a bright sun I have yet to wipe sweat off the brow. Come late afternoon, as the temperature again plunges, the heating is turned up with Midsummer a mere month or so away.

Covid 19 dislikes most the hot weather. So where is global warming when we most need it?

I find a sudden interest in gardening after a life of botanical paucity. My hands are oft stained with ink, rarely with soil. Plants under my tenancy wither and die.

Yet two days ago I planted six geraniums donated by my neighbour Pauline, who along with my partner Kitty nurtures my tentative efforts.

At the start the flowers lay supine on the soil, like corpses on the battlefield. I wake each morning excited by the miracle of them slowly stirring, raising themselves to rebirth.

Is it perhaps a metaphor, the hope for nature fighting for new life, maybe even our own?

PLANET

TUESDAY MAY 12

MORTIMER'S DEFINITIVE GUIDE ON HOW TO SURVIVE THE PANDEMIC

First – *Where are They Now??* – A series highlighting people yesterday seemingly omnipresent, suddenly, on Planet Corona, invisible. Today: Greta Thunberg, Dominic Cummings.

Meantime, there seems slight confusion as to what we should be doing right now. As an upstanding member of society (I stand up quite a lot) I've been asked by the government to make matters plain.

GOING OUT/STAYING IN: One of these is definitely advised at all times. Think of our new slogan 'Stay Alert' (which narrowly won the vote over the alternative 'Look Out for Potholes') and you'll feel better already. Be careful going out if you live in Wales or Scotland or Northern Ireland because it's different there and they might bung you in a cell.

EXERCISING: It was a one hour maximum, but now it's something else. People who have never exercised in their lives have been confused as to whether this hour was obligatory and whether this new undefined time is also obligatory and what if they have a heart attack.

TESTING: This is a very good idea.

DRIVING: It is now OK for people to go out for a drive unless it is to the places people want to visit, such as beauty spots or the seaside where you might get bunged in a cell. Feel free to drive to a lay-by on the A19 to sit quietly for three hours before returning home. People driving to the Lake District will be shot on sight.

GOING TO WORK: Work is good for you.

THE R FACTOR: Some confusion over the R factor, what it is and what does R stand for? It stands for Ronald.

WEDNESDAY MAY 13

WHY GOLF COURSES ARE IMMUNE TO PROPERTY DEVELOPERS

Golf courses are shortly allowed to reopen. Should I mention the quote popularly attributed to Mark Twain that golf 'is a good walk spoiled'?

Golfers were unlikely to be denied their pursuit for long. The people who make decisions on such things as lockdown are probably members of their local golf club. If you want a house with an unspoilt view guaranteed to remain unspoilt, buy one overlooking a golf course.

Little chance of a golf course being sold off to developers. Where would that leave the developers to play their golf?

Talking of sport, part of the new guidelines is that you can partake of a sport with one member of your household. I challenged Kitty to a bout of sumo wrestling but thus far no reply. Maybe because she gave up salt some years ago (think about it).

I've been pondering social distancing. It seems to make us more disposed to fellow humans. Many more strangers than previously now smile, say hello. Maybe two metres distance brings a new confidence, allowing our traditional British reserve to relax slightly. Less chance of invasion, which the Brits have always resisted.

Most shopping news and updates concentrate on supermarkets. I have not been in a big supermarket for a month. St. Georges Road in Cullercoats offers a splendid cluster of small shops, all highly individual. Get your hair cut, buy a painting, new double glazing, loan a library book; and there are two grocers (one also a newsagent), a greengrocer (which is also a delicatessen). I love them all. Shopping should be a social event, pandemic or no pandemic, with a sense of local connection rare in the bigger shops and online, totally missing.

THURS MAY 14

MY FUTURE BLUEPRINT FOR THOSE GHOST FOOTBALL MATCHES

As our planet grapples with its survival, Geordies wander the streets in deep contemplation. Their metaphysical questions are: (a) will them oil geezers in bedsheets buy the Toon and (b) when and how can we kick off the new season?

The former question will run and run, providing valuable copy for the poor sports writers starved of real copy. As regards the new season, I have suggestions:

Play behind closed doors but take a leaf out of TV sitcoms' books, many of whom bolster their shows with that strange animal, canned laughter.

We require not laughter but cheers, chants and those great explosions of pure joy that greet a goal (unless it's from the visitors).

We need to beware the canned laughter mistimings: the unnatural response, as can be heard when bellows of laughter burst forth at such unremarkable lines as, 'Oh dear, I've dropped the soap.'

Dovetail the sound to the action. *Howay the Lads*, *Blaydon Races* can act as general background. Whistles, catcalls and boos can be employed as required, plus 'Fat bastard!' for any opposition player over ten stone.

Can I also suggest visual support? Get season ticket holders to blow up thousands of inflatables to be placed on the seats, some in Toon scarves. Sneak in the occasional real person, (socially distanced of course) to hold the ends of the giant Toon banners which can be waved about to great atmospheric effect.

The technicalities of away supporters having their own canned audience at this stage seem unlikely. This may help the toon win occasionally.

FRIDAY MAY 15

DO I NEED TO WASH THE CAT?
WILL THE ALIENS COME SOON?

Thus we ask ourselves, what is going on? Who is to blame and why and when will they stop? Is it the end of civilisation as we know it?

What about *The Archers?* Is it the Chinese, the Russians? The Koreans? People from West Bromwich? A man in Swindon? Is it Bill Gates? The Pope? Michael O'Leary? Keith Lemon? Is it Jeremy Clarkson? Can we trust Mother Theresa?

Is she still alive?

Did I hear you cough? Can we go out, can we stay in? Is it from outer space? Where is Jacob Rees-Mogg? Why is Jacob Rees-Mogg? What about Trump's hair? Why is his mouth like a bottom? What are all the graphs? Where are all the masks?

Does whistling help?

Is it aliens? Do I need to wash the cat? Will the aliens come soon? Will they have bug eyes? Will Spielberg make a film? Can I catch this from a dog? A budgie? A goldfish? A gnat? My partner's hairbrush? Does it come up through the sink? Can it live in a beard? What does 'R' stand for? Is Captain Tom still in his garden?

What happened to Greta? Should I wear gloves? Can it live on cream buns? Can it swim through water?

When does it sleep?

What is a Covid? Why 19? Is it from the bible?

Are we being smote?

Should I get up? Can I sneeze? Was that a cough? Can I sing in the street? Where is Benítez? Boris Johnson's nurse?

The Salvation Army?

Should we pray? Should we weep? Drink disinfectant? Write to *You and Yours?*

What is to be done?

THOSE WERE THE DAYS, WE'LL SAY – AS THEY WERE. AS THEY ALL ARE

At times I think of the elderly gentleman who dreamed he was making his maiden (!) speech in the House of Lords. When he woke up, he was.

Reality can creep up and catch you unawares. It's like those times you unexpectedly catch your reflection in a shop window and think, who's that old geezer then?

As T.S.Eliot said 'Humankind/Cannot bear very much reality'. This is one reason I occasionally like penning absurdist plays. It is the most liberating writing experience I know.

Nearly two months into lockdown and we all now dream wistfully of returning to some kind of normality (as elusive a word as reality).

Human beings are born with a restless gene which means we will never be satisfied for long and yearn for something 'other'. This could be the past, the future or the clichéd fantasy, fed by endless magazines and chat shows of life styles we have been brainwashed into believing are idyllic. But you need only read of the highly 'successful' rock star, footballer or movie icon seeking help for depression, trying to end it all, or booking into rehab to realise this can be a dangerous illusion.

Here's my bet. Before too long, when it's over, we'll all be harking back wistfully to these communally rich days when we clapped together in the street, the air was pure, centenarians raised £28m by pushing a zimmer frame round the garden and unselfish, generous acts abounded.

'Those were the days.' we'll say as we seem to rush frenetically hither and thither to little purpose, coughing the polluted air. As indeed they were. As indeed they all are. They're all we've got.

THE SPECTRAL VISION THAT IS BADEN-POWELL

I awoke and saw at the end of the bed a spectral figure in a wide brimmed hat.
I'll have to watch out for that cocoa, I thought.
'Who are you then?' I asked.
'I am the ghost of Lord Baden-Powell' he replied, 'Founder of the Boy Scouts movement.'
'Didn't you write *Scouting for Boys?*' I asked.
'I did'.
'I always thought that was a bit of a dodgy title' I said. 'What do you want?'
'This new slogan, Stay Alert.'
'What about it?'
'It has been stolen from my own slogan Be Prepared. And I demand compensation'.
'I doubt that' I said. 'Anyway, they're both useless slogans. I mean, Stay at Home – we all knew what that meant. You thought, yes, I can do that. What does Stay Alert mean, except if you're next to an electric fence? Same with *Be Prepared?* When? And for what? A stampeding elephant? A plague of locusts?'
The ghost rose up and gave out a low moan. I could see right through it to the bookcase beyond.
'Compensation!' it exhaled. 'I must be compensated!'
'Hey – I just realised' I said. '*Be Prepared*, Baden Powell. Same initials, BP. Nice one. No compensation though. A queue a mile long for government grants.'
'Then I am doomed to a life of penury?' it asked.
'You won't be alone' I said. 'It could very soon be the norm.'
'Oooooh!'
The spectral vision dissolved before my eyes like a cloud of tobacco smoke. Almost time for *The Shipping Forecast*, my favourite programme, and the only one guaranteed not to mention the coronavirus.
Old Baden-Powell, eh? What's he like!

TUESDAY MAY 19

MY BIG PLAN TO SAVE THE ARCHERS – TWENTY FOUR HOUR SOAPS!

Corona claims many victims and rumours are *The Archers* could be another. Unable to tackle Covid 19, the series is already broadcasting old episodes (including the best written storyline for 30 years, Helen's and rotter Rob's break-up). The soap format on TV or radio – four or five running story lines – is no match for Corona which, if included, would be all-consuming. Producers close their eyes and hope it might go away.

The Archers is the world's longest soap (70 years). Its often ridiculous characters and dialogue were affectionately parodied even back in 1961 by writers Galton & Simpson with their satirical version, *The Bowmans*.

Tony Hancock plays local yokel Joshua Merryweather (a parody of the 'ooh-aah' character Walter Gabriel) who's written out of the script, producing a national outcry. When recalled, as compensation the actor (Hancock) is given script control and arranges for most of the village inhabitants to fall down a disused mine shaft, leaving him and his family supreme.

I have an idea. We have a trillion TV channels, mostly unwatchable. Why not mid-pandemic create a new one dedicated to non-stop 24 hours soap replays from their first episode onwards? Thus on Mondays wall-to-wall Corrie, Tuesday, *East Enders*, Wednesday *Emmerdale* and so on… around 50 episodes in each 24 hour session. And a new Radio 4 Extra(2) channel for back-to-back recordings of *The Archers* broadcast till brought up to date.

For addicts, these mega-fixes would make lockdown palatable and watching durability a challenge. How many episodes can you go before falling asleep? How long to get bang up to date? And every week, an historical quiz show on what's been seen in the previous seven days. How can it fail?

WEDNESDAY MAY 20

COVID-19 ALERT – AVOID STRING VESTS AND THE BIRDIE SONG

The government announcement that lack of taste or smell could also be symptoms of the virus has left your correspondent wondering – what else?

Could the authorities know more than they are telling? Is the secret policy a gradual release of facts to lessen the overall impact and the risk of panic in the streets?

I despatched my extensive teams of researchers to investigate. Boy – their findings are pretty scary! And remember – you read it here first.

SINGING It is now known that either singing or whistling certain songs is a clear indication that the virus may be lurking in your body. The main titles are, *'Ernie, the Fastest Milkman in the West', 'The Birdie Song', 'Chirpy Chirpy Cheep Cheep', 'Grandad'* and *'The Hokey Cokey'*. If you have sung or whistled any of these in the last two weeks you must self isolate for seven days. And cease the singing or whistling.

STRING VESTS It's unlikely there are many males left uncool enough to wear a string vest, but if there are, they need to know their problems are more than sartorial. You may well harbour the germ – your risk of Covid 19 has increased dramatically. Same advice as above, but also burn the vest/vests pronto. This is not a bad idea anyway.

CRUFTS DOG SHOW The strange desire to degrade noble canines to the level of a beauty contest has a strong link to the virus. To decrease your risk, encourage the mutt to roll around on a muddy river bank instead and put away that canine cosmetic kit.

More news as it is exposed!

PLANET  THURSDAY MAY 21

COME ALONG CHILDREN! SURELY YOU UNDERSTAND GOVERNMENT POLICY?

'Now settle down children. I know it's been a long time since you were at school, but that's no reason to get over-excited, now is it? I said, is it, Norman? That's right, no it isn't.'

'James, stop eating Susie's ear. STOP IT! If you kept two metres apart behind the striped tape, this wouldn't happen. Anyone would think you were three years old, not five!'

'What do you mean Tracey, why can't you hold Jenny's hand? Because you CAN'T. And crying won't help either!'

'Now look what you have done, you've started Amanda crying too! No, no you can't go over and comfort her, Lisa, stay two metres apart, like I told you. TWO METRES APART! I said, Jason! What do you mean, you have no idea what that means? Oh, so now you're crying as well, are you?'

'Now you've all got pens and paper and I want to see some of your lovely drawings ... No, no, Selma, you can't draw with your best friend Jane. Because that's not allowed, that's why!'

'You see what you've done now? You've upset the other children. Look how many of them are crying. Stay apart, you two, *STAY APART!!* And stop that wrestling and punching with Sean, Frank. Stop it *NOW!*'

'Yes, I know you miss the playground, Frank but that can't be helped at the moment. What's that Archie? Where are your friends Robert, William, Arthur and Colin? Well, I'm sorry but they can't be here right now. Because they will be here this afternoon instead. And no, you can't be here this afternoon, Frank no. Because ... because you CAN'T that's why. And stop crying – all of you. Please. JUST... STOP... CRYING!'

(With apologies to Joyce Grenfell)

'HE IS A DEFLATING BALLOON, THE INCREDIBLE SHRINKING MAN...'

Time for the Mortimer Master Plan. Please take notes as appropriate.

Boris Johnson has now lost it. Only a few weeks ago, post-operation, he appeared to have an epiphany, even talking about the NHS being powered by love! A Tory!

We awaited Johnson Mark 2's new Churchillian-style leadership: strength and humility in equal measure! Come the moment, come the man ... He would lead his nation forward, into the light.

Alas, no. In recent weeks his stature has diminished. He is a deflating balloon, he is the incredible shrinking man. To continue the sci-fi comparison, he is often the invisible man. Great leaders take hold of events. But events, alas, have taken hold of Boris Johnson.

And he leads a motley crew: mealy-mouthed, obfuscatory and given to uttering porkies at regular intervals. Johnson and the Johnsonites lie to us to us about all manner of things: about PPEs, about care homes provisions, about the number of daily tests (according to Radio 4's *You and Yours*, the true maximum daily figure reached is 69,000 – a long way from the fabled 100,000 every day).

Now they are doing the dirty on the very same immigrant NHS workers who each day risk their lives for us. They cock-up the return to school. And their peculiarly unattractive right-wing sees the pandemic as the ideal opportunity to crash us out of Europe minus a deal come Dec 31. Hallelujah!

So what now?

A government of national unity, that's what! Who would lead it? Keir Starmer possibly? We could ask Captain Tom to lend a hand. That dressy-up postman. Anyone with energy, ideas. Someone to inspire us. Not this abject lot.

Any ideas?

SATURDAY MAY 23

HOW MANY PANDEMICS HAVE BEEN CAUSED BY BORDER COLLIES?

Richard Kirkman, he of *The Journal* parish, says that to lead any government of national unity (see yesterday's column) we should recruit all five surviving former prime ministers, namely: John Major, Tony Blair, Gordon Brown, David Cameron and Theresa May – a curiously interesting idea. More please!

Meantime, the fourth member of our household is Rosie, Kitty's border collie, a pooch of such high IQ that I expect her update of the Theory of Relativity any day now. Rosie asked me, 'Why do you think all these pandemics attack human beings?'

'How do you mean?' I said.

'Well,' she replied 'I have yet to hear of a pandemic laying waste the global population of aardvarks or suchlike.'

'You are forgetting mad cow disease,' I said.

'Yes, but just who do you think was responsible for introducing that into the bovine population? Cows?' she said. 'Left to their own devices it is highly unlikely any species would come up with anything as monstrously devastating as Covid 19, something almost certainly created by humans, that threatens the survival of an entire race – their own.'

'Well, the dinosaurs got wiped out,' I replied.

'Meteorites.' said Rosie, 'Hardly the fault of the beasts themselves.'

'Species are dying out all the time,' I said. 'How do you explain that?'

'I think,' said Rosie, 'you'll find out that in almost every case this is down to human greed, pollution, stupidity and short-sightedness.'

'So what do you suggest, clever clogs?' I asked.

Rosie looked at me with just a slight sense of pity. That look seemed to say: for all of human history, this strange belief that you lot are the superior species. Poor, poor dears.

'Where's my grub?' she asked.

MONDAY MAY 25

THE SUCCULENT PIZZAS AND
THE WEEKLY QUIZ

The excessive winds produce a visual oddity. Not crinkly russet leaves scudding along the streets as in autumn, but in May, those same leaves, green, uncrinkly and in their prime. They are untimely ripped from their life-support – a premature death via the ferocity of these same winds.

I stand buffeted in the gale. 'Blow it all away, blow it all away,' I shout into its face, but of course, strong though it is, the wind cannot disperse the dreaded Corona. What can?

Flippantly, I find myself wondering about restaurant critics. What do they do with themselves now? Accustomed to dining out gratis on exotic foods in exotic locations, do they sit at home staring glumly at beans on toast? Are they losing weight?

New routines shape themselves in this unknown Corona territory. Thursday brings the two hour bike ride round the North Tyneside waggonways: myself, The Fidler and The Irish Rake, Tommy McClements. Someone compared us to *The Goodies*. More like *The Last of the Summer Wine* on two wheels. And the wild waggonways bring a sense of real adventure, here, on our own doorstep.

Friday brings deliciously juicy pizzas from next-door neighbour, fellow writer Pauline.

They're made from scratch, a succulence to shame their commercial counterparts. Advice in a lockdown – live next door to an adventurous cook.

Saturday brings the WhatsApp phone quiz, organised by the same Irish Rake and involving around ten teams linked to the World War One research group. It lasts three hours and important though the questions are, equally so the texted comic banter between teams, loosened by the occasional tipple.

DO YOU SEE HIM OVER THERE, THE INVISIBLE MAN?

And now I have great pleasure in announcing tonight's guest speaker. How fortunate we are to have this individual on video link to talk to us this evening.

Many of you will be eager to ask him questions. He is unique, among the most influential men in the country, a man with the ear of the powerful, a man with possibly more influence on our current government than anyone, a man behind the slogans that are said to influence each and every one of us, yet a man who NEVER SPEAKS!

Do we hear him on *Question Time?* We do not. Is he interviewed by Piers Morgan? *The Today Programme?* No. Does he appear on *Newsnight, Panorama, The Andrew Marr Show?* No. Does he grant an interview to Emily Maitlis? He does not.

Now here at last is the chance to see the man himself, hear the voice never heard!

We will hear from the horse's mouth how in a modern democracy one person can wield such power without ever uttering a word in public. Admit it – do you even know what his voice SOUNDS like? He is the Mike Ashley of politics!

Tonight it is your chance. Discover what makes him tick, why he loves visiting Co. Durham. What fascinates him so much about Barnard Castle.

Please welcome, via our special video link, Mr. Dominic Cummings ...(PAUSE).

Mr. Cummings? Are you there Mr. Cummings?

Ah ... yes, I see ... see, yes. Ladies and gentlemen I am afraid we do not have Mr. Cummings but here to answer questions on his behalf, we have a more than adequate replacement, – the – erm – the Prime Minister.

WEDNESDAY MAY 27

TIME FOR THE URINAL REVOLUTION – AND SOME MALE PRIVACY

This lockdown brings a long absence from Cullercoats Crescent Club, in normal times a fairly regular haunt and presently much missed.

A shock then to learn of the death of a Crescent mainstay, Dickie the Doorman. Traditionally clerb doormen were seen as stern, formidable figures. It's more relaxed now. Dickie's cheerful greetings and farewells, book-ended your visit. He did the rounds too, ever sociable, selling raffle and meat draw tickets, rattling change in a battered leather bag reminiscent of bus conductors (when the species existed). Dickie's conviviality is so vivid in my mind, his death seems an untruth.

The Crescent's toilets are immaculately clean. But like all public toilets, Covid may force changes. I read social distancing could see an end to that male preserve, the urinal.

Other men I'm sure share my urinal unease. Standing in a long line of male relievers, especially if those adjacent are both 6ft plus, is not the day's most relaxed moment. Are your neighbours looking over – and down?

There's a slightly disreputable sense to public male toilets, the sense exacerbated by the need to flop out the sexual member in only semi-privacy. Often these places are a bit pongy.

At St. James' Park, the long shuffling half-time queue puts you under pressure once you step up to the plate, as it were. Sometimes this pressure makes it hard to pee.

From hearsay (I hasten to add) female loos generally seem less unsavoury. Also women, even strangers, tend to chat therein, a habit most males would see as suspect.

In future, we gents, like women, may all have our cubicles and the whole urinal experience come to be seen as bizarre. Hurrah to that …

THURSDAY MAY 28

73 YEARS ON – THE NOVEL THAT'S SUDDENLY FLYING OFF THE SHELVES

My thanks to Jack Fletcher, a retired academic from Chopwell. We have in common an educational background in French and German and corresponded about various writers from said countries.

Jack sent me an essay – translated into English for the first time – by the French/Algerian novelist Albert Camus. Sales of Camus' 1947 novel *The Plague* (La Peste) have rocketed worldwide – 150,000 copies sold in Japan and ebook sales in the UK up by 3,000 percent. Not hard to see why.

The novel, set in the city of Oran during a plague outbreak, tells of the rational Doctor Rieux's attempts to find explanation and responses to the virus while the powers-that-be dither and prevaricate. *Plus ça change ...*

Like many, I read the book when a student, blissfully unaware of its pending relevance half a century later.

Camus' pre-book essay, *An Appeal to Doctors Fighting The Plague* is a mix of both practical and morale-boosting advice for the brave front-line medics. I like especially the sentence: 'Fear disposes us to accept the impact of the disease, and for the body to triumph over the infection, it is necessary to have a strong soul'.

In 2020, roll on the vital vaccine of course, but meantime, any solace to be had from Camus' spiritual words 73 years ago?

This is my 50th Planet Corona column. Lay all these columns along the A1 and – well, they would soon be blown away. Thanks to those of you who have got in touch – usually in good humour and with wit. Thanks even to the reader who fired off three quick successive salvos featuring prominently the words 'drivel' and 'rubbish'. Ta.

PLANET

FRIDAY MAY 29

'AS A TRIO, THEY ARE A POX ON OUR LAND'

And thus our weekly clapping passes into history. In our street it became more a banging and clattering, hooting and hollering, a defiant if slightly short high decibel symphony. Initially to applaud the brilliant NHS workers, it also evolved into self-support, a communal togetherness at a time of isolation and separation. We all fear loneliness and this virus has dangled before us the spectre of loneliness in extremis, that ultimate nightmare, being locked away and alone.

We long for real social interaction. Its absence leaves a hole in our lives for which no number of Zoom get-togethers can properly compensate. Covid 19 among other things has reminded us of the precariousness and fragility of life. Try this quote from the Irish poet W.B. Yeats: *All things hang like a drop of dew/Upon a blade of grass.*

It was quoted by the actor Rory Kinnear in a Radio 4 tribute to his 48-year-old sister Karina, disabled from birth. She has recently died from the virus. Kinnear's moving words, untainted by the clever artifice of actordom, stopped me in my tracks and shamed even further the opaqueness, the dishonesty, the moral bankruptcy and the hypocrisy of recent days.

I'm not sure how Cummings, Johnson and increasingly, Hancock sleep at nights. Cummings is an aberration, a scruffy unappealing, cold-bloodedly clever, conscience-free despiser of the human race which he sees as his political plaything, just as he sees himself above the tedious responsibilities of the common man or woman. Johnson has returned to his former state, a hollow opportunistic blusterer lacking all conviction. Hancock, whose half hours are rarely funny, is a smooth squirmer, wriggling his non-answer way out of all critical questions.

As a trio, they are a pox on our land and we'd be better off without them. A magic wand someone, please.

SATURDAY MAY 30

HOW WE ALL LONG FOR THE PAST; SO WHAT IF IT *WAS* RUBBISH?

It is at about this time that we human beings – impossibly contradictory creatures – grow nostalgic for the recent past and the height of the virus. As we lurch towards some kind of escape from the lockdown, I stare glumly at the roads, so recently peaceful, now slowly returning to almost nose-to-tail fume-belching traffic.

I imagine I hear the cries of the leaves on the trees. These leaves have been enjoying the rich new levels of oxygen in the air.

'Oh no!' they seem to shout as that benign level recedes and the internal combustion engine reclaims the atmosphere. 'Not back to that again!'

Did this dismay of the leaves manifest itself last week? In an unprecedented act for mid-May and still in the bright green prime of life, many of them tore themselves from their life-support trees to drift down to a premature death. High winds? Ha! Maybe!

Or possibly they'd had a glimpse of a better world only to see it snatched away. And they'd had enough.

In similar vein, I find myself yearning for the peaceful litter-free seafront of a few weeks ago. It now braces itself for a summer of casually tossed Coke cans, crisp packets, pizza trays and Big Mac cartons.

I hark back to my mid-pandemic trip into central Newcastle five weeks since, recall that meditative silence, normally the preserve of Trappist monasteries, as myself and the pigeons enjoyed a few quiet moments.

And of course, I find myself missing it.

Because that is what we do. We poor distorting humans, we miss what is not there, pandemic or no pandemic.

It's as simple as that.

MONDAY JUNE 1

ME AND JODIE FOSTER – THE FULL STORY!

Laugh-out-loud news story of the week? The pickpocket arrested at Newcastle Central Station for breaking social distance guidelines.

Meantime, Newcastle leads the country in returning to horse racing. Out they trot today at Gosforth Park, a place I have visited only once, when in the company of the Hollywood actor Jodie Foster.

No, I'm serious. I was then the arts critic for this very newspaper and Jodie Foster was on Tyneside to promote her latest film which as I recall was *Alice Doesn't Live Here Anymore*.

After the press showing, there was a hacks' trip to the races along with the esteemed actor.

This sounds glamorous but was less so. Unlike other sports, horse racing's appeal is virtually nil if you don't gamble. My philosophy has always been: gamble on life – the odds are less loaded against you than with gee-gees. And I recall my mother's words, 'I've never seen a poor bookie.'

I don't blame the horses. They're miraculous creatures which close up fill me with awe.

Onwards. I've been trying out Zoom but find it tedious: that grid of faces staring back at you like a newspaper's photo spread of victims from the latest airline crash. More relaxing is our quiz via WhatsApp, where the teams can enjoy texted banter between questions and no pressure of that massed stare.

There's endless talk of Newcastle United being bought by the Saudis, but if we're opting to sell the club's soul for a mess of pottage, why not pick that likewise potentially dodgy Chinese firm at present negotiating controversial 5G deals with our government?

The stadium chants come ready made.

'Huawei the lads! Huawei the lads! Huawei the lads!'

 TUESDAY JUNE 2

FINGERS THAT TURN THE VERY PALEST SHADE OF GREEN

Planet Corona has seen your man manifest a modicum of interest in gardening, an activity previously as remote as Malawi stamp designs.

I have a small front garden. I say small because two fat people overcrowd it.

My devotion over the years has stretched no further than a thrice annual clipping of the hedge; likewise employing an ancient strimmer over the wretched-looking lawn – first checking for possible presence of one fat person, of course.

This is an inexcusable lack of attention. Both my partner Kitty and next-door neighbour Pauline cultivate at their houses a colourful range of plants and shrubs which thrive under their loving care.

Pauline recently donated me half a dozen geraniums to replant. 'Water them every evening,' she said. 'Don't worry, they are virtually indestructible.'

I planted them deep, in soil mixed with bone meal. I watered them nightly. Two weeks on, most look as dead as a dodo.

It is my horticultural magic touch. It also highlights the conundrum. Garden stuff that people tell me must be got rid of, weeds, brambles and the like, need not a jot of cultivation or watering. Yet they run wild unaided, not giving a toss about loving care... But those beautiful flowers and plants we cherish, require compost, bone meal and much nurturing/pruning etc. Where is the green justice?

Likewise with our pandemic. The virus itself, unaided and unbidden, arrives from nowhere and runs riot through the planet. How come no antidote ever arrives unaided and unbidden and from nowhere and likewise runs riot, albeit beneficially? How come Mother Nature has no idea how to achieve an equilibrium, and leaves it to us poor lot, frantically to search for a vaccine?

THE FEAR OF THE MADDING CROWD
RUSHING INTO DISASTER

I spot a Facebook posting from my good friend at the coast, Kirstie Mackin.

'Has anyone else been watching the confirmed covid cases in your area data each day? Huge leap in cases over this weekend in North Tyneside, Northumberland and Newcastle. Over 50 in NT. In 4 days earlier last week there were only 5. Biggest leap in a short space of time I've seen in weeks. It's desperately sad. It's like that scene in the TV series *Chernobyl* where the people supposedly sat on a bridge nearby with drinks to watch it all.'

This message firms up the sense of unease felt in recent days, the fear we are making a huge mistake, indecently and recklessly rushing into a post-lockdown stage. This, despite the evidence from many other countries that acting hastily can lead to a second spike. And despite the warnings from many medical experts in the UK not to go down this premature path.

I recall that scene in '*Jaws*' where the seaside town mayor, desperate not to drive away the tourists and despite the evidence of the dangers in the waters, reopens the beaches and invites the public back in. We know the results.

Cullercoats and Tynemouth at the weekend invited them all in and they all came – in their thousands. Social distancing was spasmodic, especially in the large clusters of *yoofs* often armed to the teeth with lager.

There is that strange sense of Armageddon, of us gleefully, unknowingly, rushing towards some sort of catastrophe.

How I fervently wish I am proved totally wrong. But with so much depending on this critical period, why are we taking the risk?

THURSDAY JUNE 4

WANTED! APPLICATIONS FOR THE FIRST LITTER RESIDENCY

As the lockdown eases, litter returns in all its tacky ugliness.
I wish I understood litter and the urge to drop it. Try as I might, I cannot get inside the heads of the litterers.
In the small hours I jolt bolt upright and shout, 'Why, why?'
Why is litter much worse in this country than elsewhere?
Some countries have none.
What are a person's thoughts as they carelessly toss away that burger carton, that crisp packet, that fizzy drink can, often within sight of a litter bin?
Does leaving litter mounds in beauty spots create not a single second of guilt? Do litterers never consider taking it home in a bag? Does anyone ever look behind as they leave?
How should we deal with the litterers? Calmly remind them their actions are selfish, polluting, anti-social, unhygienic, unaesthetic, annoying, expensive? Should we lock them up? Pull out their fingernails?
In a group, do they communally agree to leave their litter, or behave individually?
Do they drop litter on their own living room carpet? Would they mind if I came and did it? If not, what is the difference? Do they ever think litter?
Phew! I'm red in the face.
Litter is one of the great social menaces. It is a self-scarring of our beautiful country. To my knowledge, no-one has yet made a feature film, written a novel, composed a symphony, drafted a play or poem or produced a documentary on the subject of litter and the litterers.
I suggest a Litter Residency. An artist given six months to unearth imaginative and creative ways of addressing the subject that has defeated all conventional thought.
Worth a try.

FRIDAY JUNE 5

A PERFECT TIME FOR THE MAGNUM OPUS... I STARE AT THE BLANK PAGE

I have been amusing myself with the world's least likely scenarios. Here they are:

A) A horse wins *Mastermind*.
B) Jeremy Clarkson gives up cars and buys a push bike.
C) Stephen Fry releases his fitness workout DVD.
D) Dominic Cummings announces: 'I have taken everyone for a ride (though not to Durham). I apologise profusely for my appalling behaviour. I resign.'

There were other possibilities: Mike Ashley selling Newcastle United to the supporters club for a tenner?

Onwards. The pandemic is the perfect opportunity for a writer to get on with his or her magnum opus, waking early to tap away feverishly at the keyboard.

Yet, this daily column apart, l have written little in the last three months. I'm relieved then to learn of several other writers afflicted with my own Corona creative catatonia.

And what of performance/publication/production? Globally, writers, actors, musicians painters and the rest sit in quiet frustration as their own creative masterpieces are denied their moment of glory. My own new play due for production at The Exchange in November now looks likely to be stalled.

No matter that the artists responsible may have been consumed passionately years long in their creation. And now suffer a silent angst. Life was never fair.

Meantime, a moment's self-reflection on Planet Corona. 'Does writing it cause you any problems?' asks a reader.

'Only on a daily basis,' I reply.

Oh, but my wit is almost Wildean in its deceptively lightweight profundity!

A daily column does offer challenges. No sooner is one finished than the next one is queuing up to be written. At that stage, I usually have not a clue as to its contents.

SATURDAY JUNE 6

A SNAKE OF MPs AND THE COMING OF THE MASKS

A photo caption in this newspaper yesterday read, 'A queue of MPs snaked around the Palace of Westminster during a vote'. And a brilliant new collective noun suddenly suggested itself – 'a snake of MPs'!

Meantime, a word about masks. Soon we shall be obliged to wear face masks on public transport, yet experts seem undecided as to whether masks are vital tools in the battle against Corona, or no more effective than a jam sandwich.

Two thoughts: firstly, advertisers – unusually – have missed a trick. Normally any blank space, be it stationary or moving is seized upon for advertising. Ads are ubiquitous: round the bottom of rugby posts, on headbands, projected onto the sides of buildings or onto football pitches, plastered over Formula One racing kits and vehicles, on taxis, on traffic islands, on peaked hats, on parking meters, on socks – the list is endless. Most Rugby League shirts are now 99 per cent advertising – hard to spot the clubs' official colours.

Secondly, I've no idea if this advertising deluge just feeds the ego of the advertisers or actually sells any of their products, but how come millions of face masks are being made totally ad-free? The admen are missing out. A face mask bearing a Pot Noodle advert may seem pretty tasteless (like the product) – but when did that ever stop advertisers?

My own support for masks in public places is psychological. Making masks obligatory brings a visual reminder we are in danger of a second spike. Recent crowds flocking to the coast, 90 per cent unmasked, brought the dangerous illusion that all was now well again.

I could almost hear the virus (if you'll excuse this mixed metaphor) rubbing its hands with glee.

MONDAY JUNE 8

POLITICIANS BLATHER. SCIENTISTS BICKER... IS OUR TIME UP?

Feverish nights follow hollow days as the shadow of this curse stalks our planet.

How do we beat this pandemic, this plague, scourge, contagion, this pestilence that has plunged our world into a medical, economic and existentialist trauma?

This dark curse makes a mockery of our claims to be strong developed societies. This is a crisis whose solution seems neither in sight nor even known.

Politicians blather. Scientists bicker. And slowly Planet Corona sucks the life-blood from Planet Earth, just as years ago, we kids sucked the lurid red colouring out of our home made suckers/lollipops, leaving nothing but sterile ice.

Is this just one small part of the universe readjusting itself? Have endless planet earths come and gone? Maybe the pandemic won't rest till it leaves humanity as a bloodless corpse, our inventions and destructions, our genius and stupidities slowly turning to zero while Mother Nature reclaims her despoiled territory? These plotlines were once the preserve of novelists and film-makers. But now we can't just close the book, or walk from the cinema as the credits roll. This time it's real. Only a blink of an eye ago, our lives were beautifully, frustratingly, exhilaratingly, bafflingly normal. We met in pubs, theatres, restaurants, we travelled to work, we wandered round crowded city centres, we packed our cases for holidays, we visited people's houses, crammed into football stadiums, we embraced friends and family. We were tactile. Now we are sterile. We can't reach out with those small vital tactile gestures.

We stand two metres distant from people whose closeness is a part of our being. We feel lost.

Yet pandemics have come and gone. Corona has come, with a vengeance. But now overstays its welcome.

Time's up, I say. But the question comes back; for whom, exactly?

 TUESDAY JUNE 9

THE POOR OLD ARCHERS – RETIRE THEM ALL GRACEFULLY

One temporary victim of corona is *The Archers*. Unable to deal with the pandemic, the world's longest running soap (on Radio Four for non-radio listeners) temporarily went off air, now returning in a new format.

The Archers always was full of somewhat unconvincing characters, a mixture of country bumpkins, cosy housewives, stupid old sods and one-dimensional dullards. In its new form, dialogue has been abandoned in favour of monologues and we hear these characters' thoughts direct-to-mike, without that essential ingredient of any drama – conflict.

You need the comic genius of an Alan Bennett or the quirky, obsessive vision of a Samuel Beckett to carry this off. Not a single Ambridge character is comic, or quirkily obsessive and their cosy often platitudinous thoughts are stretched pretty thin when left to their own devices.

The best solution, which will put audiences, writers, actors and technical staff out of their misery (and which may also already be planned in Broadcasting House) is to give our thanks to a remarkable record of seventy years continuous broadcasting, then lead the entire village off to a retirement home – one which we hope is virus-free.

Meantime a small message to the government:

"We are all human. We all make mistakes, especially in such an extreme situation. People who acknowledge this gain our respect. Not those who continually stonewall. Accept your obvious errors on lockdown dates, test and trace, care homes, Cummings. Take us on board; let us move on. At present there's a whiff of entitlement – possibly due to the many Old Etonian public schoolboys in the cabinet – that you always know best, can talk down to us and occasionally lie. Stop it."

WEDNESDAY JUNE 10

THE BODILY WITHDRAWAL FATIGUE
THAT IS GETTING TO US ALL

I have previously not given much thought as to whether I might contract the virus myself. Being of fairly robust constitution, unburdened by medication, a man who wrestles a python each day before breakfast (OK, I made that last bit up) the thought never crossed my mind.

I realise I'm over seventy, male and living in the region with the highest number of corona cases – a triple anti-bonus you might say.

None of which has made me consider the possibility of my own infection, just as I rarely consider the possibility of my own death. Death? For other people, surely!

Or, as Woody Allen succinctly put it. "I'm not afraid of death. I just don't want to be around when it happens."

I have not (or at least to my knowledge) contracted the virus. I normally wear a mask, keep my social distance and do not sneeze in public places. Nor have I manifested the normal symptoms.

Except a certain lassitude, a draining fatigue. Tasks take longer than previously, small obstacles become mountains to climb, some tasks I put aside in the hope they will go away (they don't). And suddenly I realise I am suffering an ailment that appears on none of the daily graphs but which I suspect is afflicting great numbers. I call it bodily withdrawal fatigue.

Denied the usual physical contact with all but the closest to us, we feel starved, emotionally if not physically. The importance of the hug, the cuddle, the embrace, even the slap on the back or the firm handshake only now become truly apparent.

We are hungry, we are fatigued in a whole new way, an affliction for which no cure as yet is in evidence , even on the farthest horizon.

   THURSDAY JUNE 11

ONCE WE JUST DIED. THEN WE PASSED AWAY. NOW WE SIMPLY PASS

Which usually hazardous occupation has become infinitely more secure during the pandemic? Answer – professional football manager; not a single victim over the last few months, a unique modern record.

Secondly: once people just died. Then they passed away. Now, the adverb's gone and they simply pass. Same result though.

I have participated in Zoom yoga – ancient activity meets modern tech. My yoga teacher for more than 25 years is Chrisy Edge, auntie to son Dylan. Chrisy's sensitive, knowledgeable nurturing of us mainly creaky-limbed free spirits has been a vital calming influence for this often over-excitable individual.

Yoga is an easy target for humour and we all know the maddening sense of calm, the infuriating, beaming self-sufficiency some exponents can give off. But not most. It's also often misinterpreted. Large corporations now use it to improve their top executives' productivity, which misses the point.

Nor is its objective for you to lose weight, more for the practitioner to achieve a physical and mental equilibrium and to – hang on, I'm beginning to go all po-faced.

Most yoga folk are female. In our class, an average attendance of 15 usually has three males maximum, the kind of statistic I like. A lot of men would be seen dead rather than on a yoga mat.

Now rather than gathering in a hall, pre-session we wave 'Hi!' to the images on our phone and laptop screens, curious to see the decor and living rooms of other group members. We are with them and not with them as Chrisy leads us through the 90 minute class. We face this anomaly every day in the strange new world where most human contact comes only in two dimensions.

FRIDAY JUNE 12

SHOULD CHILDREN RETURN TO SCHOOL OR STAY AT HOME? YES!

"Some people claim the government increasingly hasn't a clue what it's doing during the pandemic, so here I am, your great leader to put your minds at rest.

Education. I think this is a good idea and we shall soon introduce our Summer of Ketchup guaranteeing every child ample portions of tomato sauce. People increasingly ask for proper educational guidelines! Should children return to school? Stay at home? In answer I can say most definitely!

Bubbles – what are they? Well, some people blow them, others enjoy them in a hot bath. Our bubble means some people can sometimes go and visit some other people and even stay the night – sometimes. There are exceptions.

Second cousins twice removed, one-legged artisans, pastry cooks, retired gymnasts and sufferers from delusions of grandeur, hay fever, vertigo or an itchy nose come to mind though you may have your own ideas and the list of course is open to debate.

Social distancing has to be observed at all times. Today it is two metres, tomorrow maybe one and a half, which may be with masks or without masks, depending on where you are, the wind direction and your mother's maiden name.

What about Europe, you ask? Some people claim our plan is to keep quiet, while almost unnoticed we crash out without a deal on Dec 31, thus appeasing the party's right-wing ideologues. Some even claim this will make our already economically catastrophic situation absolutely calamitous for all but the privileged few. But I ask you – where would that kind of talk have got us at Dunkirk, or Agincourt or at Wembley in 1966? Exactly! Carry on ..."

SAT JUNE 13

STATUES OF REAL PEOPLE? THEY'RE BOUND TO DISAPPOINT

The news is now dominated by two items, the coronavirus and Black Lives Matter, the frustration of the former feeding the anger of the latter, so that in a way the two come together like a brace of cells, merging one into the other.

We feel mainly helpless in the face of this miniscule yet seemingly omnipotent bug, mocking and taunting us on a daily basis. This frustration only exaggerates the justifiable outrage we already feel at the shocking murder of George Floyd. The combustible mix spreads as quick as a forest fire, And here with this cold-blooded highly public murder is something we CAN at least effect. Huge protests take place in cities worldwide. But then more, the tearing down of statues of individuals (all male) who are seen to profit from slavery and the exploitation of the oppressed.

Why bother erecting statues of real people? Most look ridiculously pompous and are ignored 99 per cent of the time, becoming merely bombing targets for pigeons.

Humans are fallible, complex creatures, mainly a mix of good and bad that defies statue sanctification. We even have the phrase – 'to put someone on a pedestal' which implies an over-simplification of another's character.

Let's forget the whole ritual. Much better we employ our sculptors in less reverent, more imaginative tasks. Possibly fictional characters, animals real or imaginary, sci-fi critters (how about a statue of Alien in the city centre?) or modern creations such as the much loved *Angel of the North*, which speaks to us the way few statues can.

I love those floor level statues of normal folk striding out opposite Newcastle Central Station, or that strange hunched beastie looming outside Gateshead Metro. More like those please and fewer plinths.

MONDAY JUNE 15

'IMAGINE A BABY WALKER FOR ADULTS AND THERE YOU HAVE IT!'

As soon as the decision is made on new social distances, the Mortimer Virus Walker will go on the market. Orders being taken, £50 only, including postage & packing – patent applied for.

Imagine a baby walker for adults and you have it. I anticipate the walker will soon be compulsory outdoors making it impossible to get nearer to any other human being than the prescribed distance. To facilitate access to shops, public transport etc, the Virus Walker is collapsible without removal and just as easily readjusted. Extreme right-wing groups may as well stay home – the gadget makes punch-ups impossible. Meantime, I read that supplies of Marmite are limited, due to a shortage – put down to the pandemic – of brewers' yeast.

It has always struck me as curious that something with an extreme in-yer-face flavour could be vegetarian, a philosophy normally associated with the less confrontational. No matter. This being Marmite, the shortage means half the nation is booing loudly, the other half dancing for joy.

A wretched weekend, with the one-time national unity the pandemic seemed to create, now looking in shreds. It's easy to lose hope at such times, bury yourself down deep in the bed and pray the world goes away.

I do a bit of yoga to the background of Radio 3, a wonderfully eclectic classical music station (far more adventurous than Classic FM). To hear the stimulating, provocative, thoughtful, emotional, controversial music from different centuries is to be reminded of humankind's great miracle of creativity offsetting its nihilism elsewhere. For music, also read art, literature, dance, architecture, science, engineering, technology, the hula hoop and countless other wonders. Enjoy. More fun than destroying.

PLANET  TUESDAY JUNE 16

FOOTBALL IS THE MODERN OPIUM OF THE PEOPLE. LOSE IT AT OUR PERIL

Being a vulnerable sort of chap, I like to know someone out there is reading these offerings so I'd like especially to thank the following for their regular useful, often witty reactions: Colin Bowman, Kaye Cossick, Anne Olstead, Noreen Rees, Peter Stark, Terry White and Diane Whitehouse. Lack of space means I can't always respond publicly in the column but I do reply personally to those enlightened people contacting me.

Keep the messages coming!

Meantime, no-one seems to have considered the part played in the recent London riots by the long football lockdown. Groups of fans from several league clubs were in evidence. For many, mainly white, mainly young, mainly working-class males, football is an almost all-consuming passion, as it was for me over some youthful years. Its sudden unexpected removal can bring unpredictable side effects and a likelihood of frustrations spilling over into moronic and destructive behaviour.

Which is in no way to condone such terrible acts, merely more to understand them.

Luckily I escaped football addiction long before my own club, Notts County, were thrown out of the Football League, an act which in my adolescent years would have been cataclysmic enough to be almost life-threatening.

A friend, Colette, who respects total distancing and is responsible in all things recounts recently visiting an acquaintance (female) who had lost within a month both her mother and father. The friend's state was pretty abject; she had no children and was unable to arrange proper funerals. When she opened the door Colette instinctively threw her arms around her in a consoling hug.

At some moments, human compassion and kindness override the strict letter of the law.

WEDNESDAY JUNE 17

THE CORONAVIRUS IS APPALLING – WHAT BETTER COMIC MATERIAL?

Writing a daily column focusing on a single theme is a rum do. This is column 67, yet a few months ago I'd not heard of coronavirus or Covid-19.

I'd written columns for various newspapers and magazines, but always weekly and with less closely defined subject area. A weekly piece with an open brief, is a stroll in the park (and one without social distancing) compared to the present little rascal. Still, as no-one need remind me, it was my own suggestion. And it's a unique experience. A daily column sits on your shoulder every waking moment. As the day proceeds and no creative corona thought enters your mind, it regularly twists your ear, whispering: 'Well? What's it to be? Time's getting on.' The column idea took root when on day three of lockdown, I walked up to the bank counter wearing a mask – and no-one turned a hair or no-one blinked an eye.

How odd, I thought. Worth writing about. The rest, as they say is – no, no, that's a cliché and writers are told to avoid clichés like the plague.

The most important item these days is the little black notebook, accompanying me every waking moment and at the bedside overnight. It houses a jumble of small jottings, single words, phrases, quirks, witticisms, oddities observed over twenty-four hours, to be explored later.

The coronavirus is truly appalling, a mass murderer, a wrecker of lives and economies, a wreaker of havoc and devastation on a biblical scale.

What better material for comedy, satire and absurdity?

OK – that's the navel-gazing column over. Tomorrow may just contain something about bubbles and the curious ritual of spectator sport.

THURSDAY JUNE 18

ONLY TWO HUNDRED FANS?
YOU SHOULD BE SO LUCKY!

The word bubble has been given a new lease of life. For the first time, human beings can become a bubble. I have no idea who will be my bubble, nor if I will become anyone else's. I would like to report a mad rush to become the Mortimer bubble but I scan the horizon in vain. Nor have I made any move to attach myself bubblewise to any other human.

No reason.

I foresee several risks in the scheme. What if I ask to be another person's bubble and they decline? Likewise what if someone makes the same request of me and that person is someone I don't much like? And will these bubbles burst? Or will we, like singing West Ham supporters, be blowing them forever?

Meantime, the first spectatorless Premier League games have now been played. When commentators remark 'Only a couple of hundred people were allowed in the ground,' it is probably without realising that for 99 per cent of all football games in this country, a crowd of two hundred is a pipe dream.

I speak of the vast, mainly unsung amount of amateur football played not for the benefit of fans but, in the original Corinthian spirit, for the players themselves. I turned out for various amateur clubs in my city of birth, Nottingham, then Sheffield, London and here on Tyneside.

After those early Nottingham matches, partly witnessed possibly by a passing walker and dog, I would create in my imagination a national newspaper report of the game where my own performance would feature prominently.

I then believed it was preparation for becoming a full time footballer. In fact it was part of the build up to becoming a writer.

ALL TOGETHER NOW, YOU WEST ALLOTMENT FANS

And thus a cheap British drug could save the world from the Corona Curse. Or at least offer a helping hand.

Dexamethasone is a steroid. Steroids were always seen as slightly suspect medicines we were advised to stay away from. Body builders, we were told, used them illegally. The side effect was turning bodies into grossly inflated balloons.

This new drug comes from Oxford which is somehow more reassuring than saying West Allotment, though I have no idea why.

West Allotment has a lively working men's club and their football team, West Allotment Celtic, inspired by their famous Scottish namesakes, play in green hoops, the only English club so to do as far as I know … My mate Andy Waterworth is a keen fan and in more usual times often contacts me Saturday evenings to give me the latest game's report.

I've been meaning for some time to write to the football club's secretary suggesting they slightly rewrite and adopt as the fan's anthem the chorus to the country and western song *Take Me Home, Country Roads* which almost everyone knows. Substitute the words 'West Allotment' for 'West Virginia' and there you have it.

Consider for a moment, the culture of drug names and the reasons thereof. The convention is that almost all such names are long winded and the five-syllabled dexamethasone is no exception. I have it on good authority (ie a hunch) that 87 per cent of all English language words in general use are three syllables or fewer. A quick check on this paragraph reveals only two words (dexamethasone apart) in excess of three.

Need I say more?

I await (in vain no doubt) the announcement of a new drug called George.

SATURDAY JUNE 20

SO WHEN DID ONE AEROPLANE EQUAL TWO THOUSAND HOUSES?

Richard Kirkman, he of this parish, suggests the new corona drug should be called Umbrage. Everyone would feel better says Richard, after taking Umbrage … (audible groans).

And so we say a sad farewell to Vera Lynn. I enter a small plea. That we might use her death as a marker, the date on which we ended our unhealthy and debilitating nostalgia for all matters World War II and got on with modern Britain. As far as I can tell, every other nation has already done this.

To help cushion the economic effects of the pandemic £100bn is to be invested into the economy via quantitative easing. Despite an honours degree in economics, I remain mainly 'Confused of Cullercoats'. Where does the loot actually go? Is it simply swallowed up by capitalist institutions, banks and finance houses which have served us so well (!) in recent decades?

How about a few quid of it cash-in-hand to us lot – if only for a slight cheering up of a nation at present wandering in gloom and confusion?

Boris Johnson is getting £1m to repaint his plane … I know several local lads who will repaint your house for not much more than £500. Can one plane really cost the same as 2,000 houses?

Foreign Secretary Dominic Raab has lost the plot with his remarks on people's symbolic kneeling. This has nothing to do with *Game of Thrones*, curtseying to the Queen or Raab's proposal of marriage to his wife.

In a city centre street in full public view, a murderous policeman knelt for more than 9 minutes on George Floyd's neck and suffocated him. The revulsion at this act is what leads millions of people to kneel. But not Raab.

MONDAY JUNE 22

THE FAR RIGHT ARRIVED THE PREVIOUS WEEK SPITTING VENOM

Seven weeks since my last foray into Newcastle centre, then a virtually noiseless metropolis, a lonely seagull screech often the only sound breaking the skin of the silence.

But what now? Lockdown was being slowly lifted, like the raising of some creaking rusty portcullis. Portending what?

After a three quarters empty Metro (most passengers masked) I checked the potential clash of two crowds, the weekly rally for Black Lives Matter and the far right lot who'd arrived the previous week spitting venom, protesting about – well, what exactly?

The police had moved Black Lives Matter away from the potentially combustible Grey's Monument to the lower profile Times Square where several hundred people, almost all masked, all peaceful, spent a few hours listening to speeches and music. Most were white but then Tyneside is mostly white. Who would want an all-black rally on this? Newcastle Council had asked they stay away, but as several speeches affirmed, they were not going to stay away. Nor would they cause any bother. The far right, happily, failed to show at either Monument or Times Square, leaving the many police officers at both, the leisure time to do the crossword or begin writing their memoirs. I was the oldest person at the rally by about two centuries. One speaker said. 'We've got people in this crowd in their twenties, thirties and even forties'. I tried to look nonplussed. No pubs, restaurants, cinemas or theatres yet open in a city centre still trying to refind itself, shops open but awkward, large pavement arrows directing pedestrians one way and overall a slight sense of bewilderment.

Heartening then, the three singer/musicians in the entrance to Brunswick Methodist Church belting out a rousing evangelical number. Just the job.

TUESDAY JUNE 23

SO WHERE WERE THE TOON'S MISSING BLOW-UP FANS?

They said the return of the Premier League would be different but who could have guessed this? Newcastle scored three goals – almost unheard of – and Joelinton was amongst the scorers – ditto.

The new swashbuckling style and relative goals glut may see the club investigating playing long term in a locked stadium. Could that famous St. James' fans' passion, reputed to sweep the team along to greater heights, actually inhibit the players via too much expectation?

For such a suggestion I expect to be tarred and feathered and rolled out of Newcastle in a barrel.

St. James' Park looked a bit drab compared to other lockdown stadiums (or stadia for the pedants). Some weekend grounds boasted wonderfully colourful banners stretched across the stands. The Toon's were monochrome – OK, they do play in black and white – but also unimaginative. Plus we had the endless adverts for Sports Direct to thrill (chill?) the blood.

And where were both teams' inflatable fans? Newcastle is famous for its loyal fan base but when it comes to the blow-up variety, we are sadly lacking. For £20 some teams will arrange for season ticket holders to have their very own replica blow-up. We are missing out!

One idea so far not acted upon is an inflatable Mike Ashley on the centre spot at half-time with a raffle for who throws the darts.

And what about arrangements for travelling blow-up supporters? Surely a few buses could be sorted. Easier and more compact if fans travel prior to being inflated with foot pumps for the big blow-up once arrived. Fans would be deflated after the game – but no change there for Toon fans.

WEDNESDAY JUNE 24

THE STRANGE LINK BETWEEN ALAN BENNETT AND THE ARCHERS

Little wonder the BBC are bringing back Alan Bennett's series *Talking Heads* at the time of Planet Corona. Bennett's among our most brilliant writers and when millions are living in forced isolation, the monologues strike a chord. Plus which, who else to talk to in person when thus isolated?

You can discover a good deal from talking to yourself. No chance of interruption for one thing.

Compare the quality of Bennett's work (the series started last night) with that other example of the modern monologue, *The Archers*. The mainly one-dimensional characters in *The Archers* were admittedly not made for this purpose and much of the current solo offerings come over as simple-minded platitudinous guff.

In contrast, Bennett sucks us irresistibly into these small obsessive worlds of characters through which are revealed often universal truths. If that sounds portentous, *Talking Heads* is also very funny and I love titles such as *A Chip in the Sugar*, which stops us in our tracks.

My only monologue play, *A Parcel for Mr. Smith* was written specially for my son Dylan who performed it round Tyneside and at the Prague Fringe Theatre Festival.

The premise is an obsessively private man who receives an unexpected parcel and is undecided as whether to open it, a dilemma made worse when after a few days, a second parcel arrives. The obvious question some of you may (or may not) ask is what exactly do the parcels contain? I confess it's a question I've often asked myself.

Meantime, during this period of deep gloom and confusion, when the world often seems spiralling out of control, tune in to the small, beautifully observed miracles that are Alan Bennett's *Talking Heads* and feel less alone.

THURSDAY JUNE 25

EXIT STAGE LEFT, PURSUED BY... WELL, PURSUED BY NOTHING

I've decided to call it a day with Planet Corona after today's *bon mots*. It has been a glorious often madcap daily journey over almost three months but as the senna pod dealer wisely put it, all things must pass. The lockdown is easing, the daily press conferences have ended and maybe this column's natural course has been run.

Is that weeping and wailing I hear, even now are readers throwing themselves under buses, off high roofs and swallowing pure cyanide? Or simply saying 'Oh' and turning the page?

Such a voluntary end is novel for me. Usually I get the sack (including from this very newspaper many years ago).

My relationship with *The Journal* goes back 50 years and though I've written for many other publications, *The Journal* has always been special.

Coronavirus has not gone away, nor is it likely to for some time, despite the changing behaviour of a a sizeable number of people. I fear the virus' latent dangers, the sense of its power, briefly dormant, lurking in the shadows, awaiting its next deadly move.

On Cullercoats seafront, I see the swathes of trippers. With pubs reopening I imagine the Bigg Market, 10pm on a Friday night. What relevance will social distancing have there?

Plus that image from the film *Jaws*, where encouraged by the sleazy mayor determined not to lose tourist income and despite the best scientific advice, holidaymakers flock back to the beach while a solitary shark fin is seen moving through the waters offshore. We know the rest.

But hey – enough doom and gloom! It's been a hoot. And thanks to all of you for (however occasionally) taking part. We will, somehow, meet again.

PLANET  WEDNESDAY JULY 1

GUESS WHO? YOU MUST HAVE MISSED ME TERRIBLY!

'Hang on Mortimer, did you not you bring this column to an end a week ago?'
'I confess I did.'
'So what are you doing back here?'
'What I'd like to tell you is that since that day I have been utterly besieged by hordes of fanatical readers bewailing loudly that their lives are impoverished and incomplete without the regular dose of Mortimer pandemic absurdity.'
'Surely that can't be true?'
'You're right, it's not true, but it's what I'd LIKE to tell you.'
'The truth being?'
'A man from Ebchester sent me an email.'
'That was the true extent of the fan mania?'
'Actually, I jest still. I confess to being heartened by a supportive response and request to bring the column back in some form.'
'Are you always this indecisive?'
'No argument about that whatsoever. I am always, always this indecisive. Do I make myself perfectly clear?'
'What are the plans now?'
'I calculate Covid-19 still has sufficient resources to deal with two columns a week.'
'Which will be those unlucky days?'
'Wednesday and Saturday.'
'Is the seemingly endless pandemic not now beyond a matter for humour?'
'Ah, but remember the saying, 'Laugh, though the game is up.'
'Who said that exactly?'
'I think it was me.'
'Did anything else change your mind?'
'I was watching what was supposedly a football match between Newcastle and Man City on Sunday and found myself scribbling a note.'
'The note said what?'

'I quote: "The Man City half of the pitch is such an unused area of grass, it may as well be sold off to property developers."
I considered this quite droll and worth putting in a column.'
'Any other thoughts of deep comic profundity strike home?'
'Thus far, no. Yet they're out there somewhere.'
'No doubt. Well, don't let me keep you.'
'I wish someone would keep me.'
'More of this stuff on Saturday, I assume? To coincide with the pubs re-opening?'
'You see? The absurdity comes ready-made!'

 SATURDAY JULY 4

RING OUT THE BELLS! PLAN 'A' TO COMBAT THE BEACH BOOZERS

As we move to post-lockdown, North Tyneside beaches have witnessed various drunken punch-ups (the plural strictly should be 'punches-up' as 'up' has no plural, but only a pedant would mention that). The battlers are predominantly young, white and male and most lug with them a box or plastic bag of booze. The majority being poetry lovers, they can be heard reciting in unison the erstwhile poet laureate John Masefield's famous lines, 'I must go down to the sea again/The lonely sea with me mates/Where all I ask is a dozen cans /And a punch-up to follow. Just great.'
A Cullercoats petition to ban alcohol from the beach was signed by more than 5,000 fed-up locals, including one African grey parrot.
Cllr Carl Johnson at this week's cabinet meeting said that while it was legal to ban dogs, the same was not possible with booze. Hmm.
Some lateral thinking required here, I pondered.
Thus the Mortimer idea. If you can't ban booze, unban the dogs. Train said canines to react to and deflect those reeking of alcohol and raising the fists. The odd pulled-down bather or ripped trackie bottom should be sufficient deterrent to deflect the attention of would-be combatants.

Also, church bell ringing has been ravaged by Covid-19 and many churches stay silent. The sound of church bells is among the most comforting and soothing known to humankind and another possible solution to the drunken beach maulers is to have a recording of the same campanologists peeling out from St. George's Church across Cullercoats Bay and the Long Sands. How could you carry on flailing about to that background?
'The taverns will be full of gadabouts making merry this evening. I am tempted not by the sweetmeats within. A dram in exchange for the pox is an ill bargain indeed.'
Not my words, but from the diary of Samuel Pepys, 1665 and sent to me by my son Dylan. Prescient, I would call it.

WEDNESDAY JULY 8

ARE THE PUPILS OF ETON LEFT TO ROAM THE STREETS? THOUGHT NOT

Anyone heard anything of the R number of late? Me neither. Meantime, we can now get sozzled in pubs, eat out, have a haircut, get our nails painted, but kids can't return to school. Here's how we treat the youngsters. Lock them up at home for three months until levels of frustration and boredom are maximum, then push them out into the street, with no idea of what they should do next. Why not the discipline and challenge of school to stimulate and focus them? After all, they're the least likely to contract the bug.
Sorry – no can do. Oh, look, some of them are indulging in anti-social behaviour.
Kids today – now in my time ...
One thought – what about the private schools? Are the pupils of Eton left to roam the streets? Doubt it.
Meantime, Donald Trump, the orange maniac, says he wouldn't mind wearing a mask and – in the nearest the man is ever likely to get to a sense of humour – adds he might be mistaken for the Lone Ranger.
Except the Lone Ranger wore an eye-mask, which let's face it is no use at all either disguisewise or coronawise.

Did no-one tell Trump?

Anyway, I'm all for the maniac wearing a mask. The more of him that's covered up, the better.

Hurrah – a rescue plan for theatres. As a writer, critic and plain audience member I've been going cold turkey without live performance. Its absence is a hole in my life the size of Jeremy Clarkson's ego.

I love cinema – my jaw drops at the technological magic of film which can do anything. But nothing compares to taking your seat in a theatre audience, real human beings but a short distance away, convincing us that they are not themselves, not here, not now; an alchemic metamorphosis with the added spice that the actors may do something wrong – impossible in a film.

Thanks to those pointing out the 'Samuel Pepys' extract (Saturday) is in fact taken from the clever pastiche, *The Secret Diary of Samuel Pepys, aged Ten & Three Quarters* by Julian Dutton. Happy to be fooled!

SATURDAY JULY 11

THE THREE STOOGES? THE GOODIES? THREE MEN IN A BOAT?

Early in lockdown, at the instigation of my friend The Fidler, myself, himself and Tommy the Irish Rake embarked on 12 mile bike rides along the secret delights that are the wagonways of North Tyneside.

And by George, we're still at it! Each Thursday we cycle a two hour journey along these therapeutic arboreal splendours, three men of a certain age (mature age certainly, though Tommy the Irish Rake boasts a relative juvenility of only 50+). I think of us somewhere between *The Goodies, Three Men in a Boat* and the loveable ragbag trio in *Last of the Summer Wine*.

The Fidler, first name Alan, carries secateurs with which he trims overhanging foliage en route. He sees this as a natural duty to the human race and elsewhere in the week devotes several hours to same task. I admire such functional eccentricity and give him the nickname, Alan Shearer, though despite his age, he has considerably more hair than the legendary Newcastle number nine. His response is the normal deadpan.

Frequent stoppages come also from Tommy the Irish Rake, who has a photographer's compulsion regularly to stop and photograph a dandelion, a puddle, or a tree that resembles Charles de Gaulle. Last week we ratcheted everything up and took an all day 35 mile circular expedition, from Whitley Bay, up through Bedlington and back. The Fidler and I came prepared with sandwiches, coffee, chocolate and fruit. The Irish Rake had a small pack of tea biscuits and wore a ton of clothing.

On we cycle.

This week I ventured back into the world of licensed premises, Tynemouth Working Men's Club, where social distancing proves little problem.

Despite slurping the odd Pinot Grigio at home, in almost four months I had not put to my lips a single pint of my more normal cask ale.

This may explain why the brace of pints left the sense of a distended gut and a sensation of having swallowed the equivalent of Lake Windermere. The next morning I also felt hung-over.

Is this incident, like the pandemic itself, trying to tell me something?

WEDNESDAY JULY 15

WHY FOOTBALL COMMENTATORS ARE SENT NO JAM TARTS

Consider the patterns of our two national sports during the spectator-free pandemic. For football it's the recorded crowd noise, the inflatable or cut-out figures, the giant logo banners in the stand. Cricket, back with the world's first pandemic test match, considers itself more sophisticated. No amplification, no mock spectators. Yet for many, accustomed to county matches with a mere sprinkling of the faithful in an otherwise empty ground, it's familiar territory.

Football has become a more civilised game without the crowds. Fewer fouls or histrionics. Less of the fierce scowling from some goal scorers at that moment when pure joy is the natural reaction. I like all this.

The best way to experience either sport at the moment is via the radio. Football broadcasts on Five Live are little changed; easy to imagine packed stadia when listening to the full sound effects background.

And it's easy often to forget the reality when listening to cricket's *Test Match Special*. The Barmy Army apart, cricket crowds' usual reaction to dot balls (those with no runs accruing, which constitute the majority) is fairly muted. Only in the silent response to a boundary or a captured wicket do we realise the new artificiality. I also value cricket commentators' wit and wisdom and how they wander less frequently into clichéville. Old ladies send these cricket cognoscenti cream cakes and jam tarts – difficult to imagine the same with football counterparts. Nor do football commentators wax lyrical about a passing cloud's similarity to the Taj Mahal.

Exclusive news on a new TV game show about to be launched, '*Mask or No Mask*' will be hosted by whichever gleeful and vacuous celebrity takes the lowest fee.

Here's how it works. Four contestants wearing masks are each asked a series of general knowledge questions. Every time the answer's right, they get a point. Wrong, and they need to remove their mask for twenty seconds while a Covid carrier chases them round an obstacle course, coughing energetically. Top prize, £100,000! Booby prize (possibly) – the virus!

PLANET Corona

SATURDAY JULY 18

YOUR PLAY IS POSTPONED! GO FORTH AND PICK UP SOME LITTER!

I have taken delivery of a litter-picker. The beautiful Cullercoats coastline is uglified by the presence of the same litter and here is an item which I am hoping may make me feel marginally useful. Of late, I have not felt useful.

I cheer myself up with a quip:

THE QUEEN:

Phillip, where is the litter-picker?

PHILLIP: I'm afraid I had to let him go.

Here now is No. 56 in Planet Corona Curios you may have missed. Apparently, The Jawastra Culture Movement in Indonesia, in an attempt to help people deal with their coronavirus stress, is urging them to swear creatively.

My reaction?

What a ******* stupid idea! It's a load of *********! I've never heard such **** in my life!

Boy – do I feel better for that!

(Well, actually, no.)

I think back 400 years, when the previous Elizabethans faced a similar crisis to our own. In 1603 the bubonic plague saw every theatre close for 14 months.

William Shakespeare, Christopher Marlowe and others of that ilk were left to twiddle their thumbs, write hack travel articles, or advertise the latest brand of collar ruffs. They did survive, as will I. I do have a full-length play written and booked for a November run – now delayed until who knows when. I fantasise about how many people are weeping and wailing over such news but find these people not particularly in evidence. And I ask myself, why should they be?

I unwrap the litter-picker and give it a trial run along the seafront. Its orange claw shows the litter no mercy. It hoists its victims in the air then drops them into my bag. It reminds me of the long tentacles of the Martian machines in Spielberg's *War of the Worlds* collecting up humans.

The one hour's lo-tech activity is good for the soul, both meditative and worthwhile. And indeed I am a lo-tech creature, out of sync with much of our hi-tech brave new world.
This connection to the earth leaves me feeling just slightly, marginally, of some use. But will it last?

PLANET Corona

WEDNESDAY JULY 22

ARISE SIR TOMMY. HANG ON, WHERE ARE YOU GOING?

It's rare these days for the Queen to knight anyone older than herself but there she was, laying the sword on the shoulder of Capt. Tom Moore, the one person in the UK whose age EVERYONE knows.

The ceremony is normally indoors, full of pomp and the recipient is expected to kneel.

All changed for young Tommy. You may remember he planned to raise £1,000 for the NHS when he started walking round his garden. He ended up with £33m – a 330,000 per cent leap. That's about standard for budget forecast increases in this country – take HSR2, road building or any major public construction scheme – but normally it's loot being spent not donated. I think the honours list should be abolished but make the exception in Tommy's case.

I doubt he was seeking rewards for his perambulatory heroics, nor is this fame likely to turn his head and lead to a life of hard drugs and easy women. Unlike most famous people, he seems not to give a fig about image or adoration.

My admiration for Tommy-boy shot up tenfold when I learnt a little publicised fact about his Royal visit.

The Queen had offered to host tea for him, but he turned her down. That's right – he snubbed the Queen.

Apparently he had already made other plans with his family. Such regal invitations are not a spur-of-the-moment matter; not just a case of putting out an extra chair and plate. Protocol, security, schedules etc demand forward planning. The invite would have come as part of the package.

I imagine him opening the letter.
'I've been invited to Windsor Castle to get a knighthood.
Tea and cakes with the Queen after.'
'That's nice, Tommy. We normally meet for tea and buns in Bedford on a Friday. We'll cancel it that week, then.'
'No, no, that's alright. I'll get back in time. I'll tell her I'm busy.'
The world is full of people whose wildest ambition would be to be invited to tea with the Queen.
The world though, is not full of people like the truly remarkable Sir Tommy Moore.

SATURDAY JULY 25

MORE MUSINGS ON THE ART
AND CULTURE OF THE LITTER PICKER

A word on the Test series between England and the West Indies, played on Planet Corona in front of 20,000 enthusiastic if mainly empty seats.
Not only do the Windies team smile more than most modern professional sportsmen, during the previous test, they also (if briefly) broke out into song.
I think of the Brazilian footballers, who – heaven forbid – seem to enjoy it all. They run out onto the pitch linking hands; sometimes each player is hand-in-hand with a child, not a scowl in sight.
Meantime, the pandemic has resulted in the number of Beefeaters at The Tower of London being reduced. I ask myself, does this constitute a victory for the vegetarians?
Spurred on by one of the coast's activists, Joan Hewitt and the small benevolent army of Tynemouth litter pickers, I am now well into my own Cullercoats mission, venturing forth most days for one hour, brandishing my Hillbrush picker. By the time I reach the seafront this predatory beast is already snapping its jaws in excitement and will not rest until my bag is full of society's discarded detritus.
In former times, only park keepers would collect litter, armed with the kind of metal spike with which toreadors torment bulls.

How did this spike work with litter on concrete? Or was this failure the reason it became redundant and was overtaken by the Hillbrush version?

Few people know this new version was invented by the comedian Benny Hill. Or maybe it was the racing driver Graham Hill. Or possibly the erstwhile footballer-cum-pundit Jimmy Hill. Whichever, they were definitely in partnership with the furry entrepreneur, Basil Brush.

The popularity of these modern items speaks both bad and good of our society; bad, because they are regrettably needed, good, because it is the kind of communal activity that gives you hope. I can recommend it as good for the soul – either in isolation or a group. Each single litter item hunted down, clamped, lifted and plonked in the bag brings a small thrill of victory. Die, litter, die!

WEDNESDAY JULY 29

IS THE MUSTARD SANITISED?
THIS AND YOUR OTHER VITAL QUERIES

It obviously needs someone of my intellect, wealth, good looks, generosity, decisiveness, wit and gargling skills to clarify the current Covid 19 situation for you. So here goes.

Some of you seem concerned over the easing of lockdown just as globally the number of corona cases is rocketing. A good point.

Now – onto social distancing; people ask should we all keep (a) one metre apart (b) two metres apart, or (c) one metre plus? And what does 'plus' mean? An inch? A mile? Indeed!

Who, you ask, can visit whom, when and where and for how long and should you wash in Harpic first? Are we allowed sleepovers and if so, do we need to bring our own pillows? And do we sleep in a mask? Good questions, all!

Do second cousins thrice removed count as close relatives and can you share a shower cubicle with them? Is it obligatory? Should you both wear a mask? Are there any waterproof masks? Excellent questions!

Can I go on holiday now? And wear a mask? Can I come back from holiday? Still in a mask? What do I do when I get back?

Am I locked in a room for two weeks? Dipped into a septic tank then asked to wear a hospital gown that exposes my bottom? Do I buy a new mask? All relevant queries!

What about pubs? Why are they meant to be open but most of them aren't? And what of restaurants? Are we meant to support them or just eat lettuce leaves at home because we're all so fat? Is the mustard sanitised?

A reader is worried about his deteriorating eyesight. Can he have Dominic Cummings' optician contact in Barnard Castle? It's not expensive – word is you get away scot-free.

What about my aged aunt in a care home? Do I need to shout through the window or will they let me in? Will they let me out?

How long will the pandemic last? Another half hour? A millennium? Till Tuesday? Forever? Longer?

Thank you for those enquiries. Your concerns are important to me. Goodbye.

SATURDAY 1st AUGUST

'LIKE A CHUBBY CHEEKED BABY. YOU WOULD EXPECT HIM TO GURGLE'

Footie news this week leaves me pondering which will come first, the end of the pandemic or the eventual sale of Newcastle United? Two endless roads ...

I also ponder, where is Dominic Cummings? Since The Weasel's outrageous and unpunished behaviour ('We are all in this together,' remember), he's gone to ground, where I assume his Machiavellian activities continue out of sight.

I also wonder about the Two Tubbies. One pandemic curio is that for the first time it gives us both a portly UK Prime Minister and a portly US President, each sporting a blond haystack.

Is it relevant that the US and UK are (a) the two fattest nations on earth and (b) world leaders in Covid 19 cases. Who says we're finished?

Taking a cue from our great leaders, our two nations gradually junk themselves to yet higher levels of obesity, which, in a telling

partnership with Covid, could well wipe us all out. Nice one.
Fat leaders are rare in the West. Few are bald either. Eisenhower was an exception in hirsute shortcomings and this side of the pond, Douglas Home and Clement Attlee come to mind. I know not a single present world leader both fat AND bald.

North Korea's Kim Jong-un does his best. He's a chubby-cheeked baby who you would expect to gurgle rather than talk. He's not bald, though his outrageous haircut stands in sharp contrast to his country's otherwise strict orthodoxy.

The pandemic sees the latest UK car production figures at the lowest in 66 years. Nobody seems to be cheering except me. Let's have far fewer cars on the road, say I. I contribute towards the cost of my partner Kitty's car but haven't owned one for 30 years.

Churning out endless new cars is accepted as a good thing, despite effects of pollution, congestion, road deaths, physical and mental health.

Here's our big chance. One possible benefit of Covid 19 is a chance to reappraise how we live our lives. Let's start with reduction in car use. On your bike. Go on.

WEDNESDAY AUG 5

LARGE PEOPLE AND LARGE VEHICLES – THE WORLD IS GETTING HEAVIER

The chances of contracting the pandemic apparently increase by 50 per cent if you are obese. This seems mathematically logical, as most people who become obese also increase by about 50 per cent. Airlines are already having headaches squeezing the obesities (as I call them) into a normal seat. A more bizarre fact this week is news of some churches' dilemma when one obesity marries a second.

The aisles are not wide enough for a brace of obesities and pews are having to be removed. One answer might be that the brace of obesities walk up the aisle not next to each other but sideways, a soft shuffle towards the altar. Each could simply turn their head 90 degrees when asked to say 'I do' etc. They could then shuffle their way back out again when the ceremony is complete, before tackling the high calorie buffet.

Largeness is in the news. Statistics show that 40 per cent of new vehicles sold in the UK (people apparently still buy cars mid-pandemic) are SUVs.

SUV is such an ugly acronym that it is never spoken but always pronounced as three separate letters.

The vehicles themselves are also big ugly lumps and often a manifestation of the modern males' attempts to appear macho. Eco-disasters on many levels, (including fuel guzzling) they muscle their way down High Streets whose two lanes of parked cars bring a 50 per cent reduction in width – so be prepared to reverse 500 yards if faced with an oncoming SUV.

At traffic lights they loom in your rear mirror like some frightening dark behemoth, blocking out the light through your back window.

Such is my distaste for this kind of vehicle that I instantly (and of course unfairly) imagine their owners as fat, reactionary, red-necked, opinionated and loud. Oh, and male. Oh, and fierce supporters of Brexit.

In decades to come (if we're still around) and attitudes slowly change, we may view those driving SUVs with the same kind of curiosity and incomprehension we now reserve for that small minority still smoking sixty fags a day.

PLANET *Corona* SATURDAY AUGUST 8

EVERYTHING AT GREGGS IS COLD – CAN IT BE A METAPHOR?

A rare bus journey to Newcastle city centre – yet it is not the real Newcastle City Centre. Consider the Greggs' Store in Clayton Street.

'Are those vegan bakes warm?' I ask.

'Sorry' comes the reply. 'They are not'.

'How about the vegan sausage rolls?'

'No, they're not warm either.'

'OK.' I briefly abandon my high principles. 'What about the steak pie, the meat sausage rolls, the pasties?'

'Everything is cold,' comes the reply.

This is a disappointment, but also a metaphor. This great city, this vibrant, sometimes vulgar, irreverent, maddening, irresistible, hard-edged, unique city normally pulses with warm blood.

On this day, battered by months of the relentless and merciless pandemic, struggling to regain its true heartbeat, it is anaesthetised, it is on life support.

Witness that jewel in the city's cultural crown, Tyneside Cinema. Normally it has a brilliant all-day film programme, its many cafés and bars buzz, its al fresco café in High Friar Lane, an ethnically diverse meeting place. Now, all silent, locked, as cold as a Greggs' pasty.

The usually busy Grainger Market, a Victorian gem that lives comfortably in the 21st century has the pallor of a ghost. Stall holders – those still in evidence – stare glumly along the almost empty aisles.

Only one open-plan café remains operative, its solitary customer slowly munching a cream sponge slice.

It is a city centre that began tentatively to emerge from lockdown, only to see it snatched away by confusion, indecision, obfuscation and procrastination, the growing sense that nobody knows how or when all this will end.

I tell myself this is all a test from which we will either emerge wiser, more compassionate and less prone to destructive negative behaviour, or we will not emerge at all and will not deserve to do so.

On the 308 bus to Whitley Bay there's an official sticker: 'Please Go upstairs if You Can'. The lower deck is well sprinkled with the masked elderly – for many such an ascent would be formidable if not impossible. On the upper deck there's a gaggle of young'uns, high spirited, unmasked.

WEDNESDAY AUGUST 12

SO WHERE ARE ALL THE PIES, MR NICHOLSON?

The pandemic has seen a large and welcome rise in bike use. Most bikers now seem lean, fast and lyrca-clad, bent over the dropped handlebars with serious intent and reaching alarming speeds. They rarely whistle.

They whizz past my bike in a blur. I stupidly press a bit harder on the pedals, as if keeping up were an option. Four decades ago, maybe ...

Alas, reality has to be accepted ... I shall never wear the yellow jersey again.

In my early biking days round Cullercoats, my conveyance was an old black butcher's bike in whose front carrier I would plonk my infant son, Dylan. This combo was a regular sight at the coast but inevitably Dylan outgrew the carrier. 'I think you'd better get out now.' I eventually said. 'You are twenty-six.'

Dylan now whizzes about on his own bike, again at great velocity and some years ago cycled the Grand Canyon for charity.

Whistling occasionally, I hope.

I eventually gave my butcher's bike to Nicholson's, the famous Whitley Bay Butchers, who smartened it up. It now sits outside their Park View premises advertising the shop.

Nicholson Snr. promised me a 'fair few pies' in return but by the time the bike was in situ, he had gone to the great abattoir in the sky. It felt mean spirited to bring it up and my occasional pie comes from an inferior source.

A succession of bikes has followed, always Raleigh, part of my loyalty to the Raleigh factory based in my home city, Nottingham.

I bought an extra Raleigh bike during a month spent there a few years ago when writing the book *Made In Nottingham*. Emotionally unable to sell it, I brought the bike back and gave it my fellow Cullercoats scribbler, Tony Henderson, who rides it yet. Meantime, the pandemic-induced rise in biking sees some local authorities changing traffic layouts in response. As ever, many motorists are up in arms over any restriction to their 'freedom', but I sense the car's total road dictatorship may eventually be under threat. For which you can mainly thank Corona. Funny old world.

 SATURDAY AUGUST 15

ARE ONE-LEGGED CROSS DRESSERS MORE LIKELY TO BE CARRIERS?

Recent statistics on just who has had/might have had/should have had the virus have been confusing. Are the 5,000 dead or alive, for one thing? Luckily I have interviewed a government leading expert, Mr Bonkers, to answer your queries.

Q. Mr Bonkers, how many people have contracted Covid-19 in this country? Estimates vary from just eight right up to five million.

A. This depends on just what exactly you define as the cause of death. Several people confirmed as having died from Covid-19 are now known to have met their end through different causes.

Q. Can you give some examples?

A. One supposed victim from Runcorn was later proved to have seen sat on by a horse. A woman in Basingstoke similarly originally placed was then confirmed as having swallowed a parrot – an African Grey. These are easy mistakes to make.

Q. Categories are also confusing. Are one-legged cross dressers from East Africa more likely to be carriers?

A. One eminent research paper suggests so. Then again, another leading expert has pinpointed bald Turkish barbers as a high-risk category.

Q. What exactly are my own chances of contracting the virus if I sit in a pavement café in the centre of Newcastle eating a cheese and hummus baguette?

A. This depends entirely on the cheese.

Q. Sneezing is said to increase the risk of the virus being passed on. What about whistling?

A. A good question. You could probably whistle something slow – say *Fantasia on a Theme by Thomas Tallis* and get away with it. I'm not sure you would be as lucky with a rapid piece.
Q Such as?
A. Well, Rimsky-Korsakov's *Flight of the Bumble Bee* comes to mind.
Q. Have you ever known anyone whistle Rimsky-Korsakov's *Flight of The Bumble Bee?*
A. We have to be aware of all eventualities.
Q. What about wearing a woolly hat?
A. There's always that of course, yes.
Q. What general advice would you offer the public?
A. Stay in unless you go out.
Q. Thank you, Mr Bonkers.
A. Always pleased to help.

WEDNESDAY AUG 19

THE IRRESISTIBLE APPEAL OF SKEGGY BEACH

Readers seem occasionally unaware of what is true and what I make up. This has led to the odd moan, such as with my recent news that for social distancing purposes, some brides and grooms could only walk side-by-side if the church widened the aisle by removing pews. Fattist humour, claimed some.

Yet the item is true. See what you make of the following piece of news: medical authorities are shocked by the recent revelation that the most infectious part of the body for Covid 19 transmission is the elbow, regardless of whether the skin is covered or not.

Thus, all those people doing the seemingly safe elbow greeting may have passed on the virus or contracted it themselves. This is an estimated 35 million souls and hospitals are gearing themselves up for a second, third, fourth, fifth and sixth strike which will rapidly overwhelm them. Discerning readers will have identified the above as a product of Mortimer's convoluted imagination and entirely fictitious.

What is true is that bats are now established as the source of the pandemic which worldwide has already claimed more than 750,000 lives. The closest match to the virus has been found in the horseshoe bats in Yunnan, Southern China.

If you're booked to holiday there, I suggest a switch to Skegness. Skeggy has the world's most faraway low tides.

To go for a low tide paddle at Skeggy requires you (a) buy a compass, (b) leave a grid map reference with the coastguard, (c) hire a professional guide and (d) stock up with essential provisions including smoke flares.

Back to bats; novelist Bram Stoker and endless filmmakers adapting his book, *Dracula*, have given bats an unjustified bad press.

Until I actually saw a bat, I expected them to be terrifying creatures with huge wing spans.

Bats are little bigger than a donut and give off a tiny squeak – a reality at odds with a blood-sucking creature capable of becoming a fanged Christopher Lee. Nor is the adjective 'batty' complimentary. There is no scientific evidence of bats being mentally unstable. This is true.

SATURDAY AUGUST 22

'IN THE MADNESS OF CORONA, IRONING SOOTHES THE SOUL'

Life is turned upside down and all of us with it. There's chaos, hotly pursued by absurdity, incompetence, blustering and bringing up the rear, a sense of comic tragedy.

Education is wonderful. Especially if you're locked out of school for six months, then told your exam assessments have been sabotaged by a piece of hi-tech infantilism known as an algorithm. 'Resign!' we scream at the feeble and bamboozled education minister, the dodgy building minister who surrounds himself with shady deals, plus the government special adviser who writes his own rules and is given the platform of the Downing Street garden, metaphorically to blow contemptuous

raspberries at us all – and turns up thirty minutes late to do so.
'Resign – blaggards!!' we shout at them all.
'Shan't!' they shout back, shamelessly – these three white male walking disasters. Nothing changes. Except we're offered a month of half-price dinners (Mon–Wed only).

Meantime, when he is seen – which is rarely – the PM goes on another publicity walkabout in a fudge factory or some such. In the photo-op, wearing a blue plastic cap, he gives a thumbs-up grin to the cameras, declaring the fudge to be world class – along with everything else.

We yearn for some kind of normality, yet normality seems to have fled the planet.

Thus I seek solace in a simple, uncorrupted task – that of ironing three shirts. I think of my mother, who would iron even underpants and socks.

In the madness of Planet Corona, ironing soothes the soul. Were I faced weekly with an ironing pile the size of Everest and surrounded by four endlessly screaming kids, the feeling may be less benign, so I count my blessings.

I love the soft hiss of the iron as it passes over the troubled creases. They vanish miraculously. I love the warmly comforting aroma that rises from the ironed shirt and the occasional steam, hovering briefly like early morning mist over a field.

What has this to do with Corona, you ask me? I reply that all is connected and like everything else, ironing is more than just itself.

WEDNESDAY AUGUST 26

DOING THE CAMEL CONTORTS YOUR LIMBS INTO A PICASSO PAINTING

Zoom was a word rarely used pre-Corona. As was furlough outside the USA. Now, in six months, furlough has become a fully paid-up member of the common language club.

Six months is a lot of Planet Corona columns and if you laid all those words end to end – well, why bother?

In convivial company last week, one person asked, 'When do you think you'll stop, Mortimer?' and another came back with 'When he gets it right, presumably.'

Actually I just invented that entire last paragraph, but it goes to show.

Back to Zoom. I mentioned previously how I found it off-putting to see that grid of faces onscreen, like a newspaper spread showing victims of an air crash.

Yet now I use Zoom for weekly yoga sessions which I do on my mobile. When we are ready in our various domestic locales, teacher Chrisy Edge greets then mutes us all, mainly I suspect to cut the sound of my own creaking bones, or my yelp of pure despair when she says, 'Next we'll do the Camel' – a position requiring limbs to contort into shapes which would look odd even in a Picasso painting.

'Time to lie down,' says Chrisy. I lie down but realise I have placed the mobile on top of the chest of drawers. It is now out of sight. I prop it up on the carpet where a contortion of the neck (not recommended in yoga) brings it into view.

'Time to lay on our tummies,' says Chrisy a few moments later. I can no longer see the phone, neck contortion or not. Maybe I could hold it up in the air? I do so.

'Now turn over and place both hands under your back for the Fish,' says Chrisy.

I wedge the mobile up on a high bookshelf but in doing so touch the screen and Chrisy becomes a tiny square in the corner.

'Chrisy!' I yell, but I am muted.

'Dog With Leg Up,' says Chrisy. This becomes Dog With Leg And Head Up, otherwise I can't see a thing.

An hour later – all done. How calming this yoga is. I zoom off.

PLANET Corona

SATURDAY AUGUST 29

THE VIRUS HASN'T GONE –
IF ONLY THAT MAN WOULD

In his convention speech, President Trump – and nausea and deep revulsion rise up in me even to type those two words – chooses as always to call Covid 19 'the China virus' in yet one more calculated insult to a nation he hates. Have you ever heard the man say 'coronavirus'? You may as well wait for him to say 'I am sorry' or 'I was wrong'.

You may as well wait for some condemnation of, or reference to the incident in Illinois: a black man shot by police seven times in the back, leaving him paralysed. You may as well wait for Trump to acknowledge that he has led this wondrous nation of ideas, energy, go-getters and political gullibility into the most severely divided, violent state we can remember.

Instead, with US corona deaths pushing 200,000, he parades his family in public to tell the world how good he is; he pushes forward his Vice President and lackey, Mike Tuppence, feebly to claim conditions would be even worse under Joe Biden. Trump, you see, is sorting it.

It matters little that his highly unattractive mouth puckers into an anus, or that his name is a synonym for flatulence.

What matters is that he is narcissistic, emotionally cold, creatively sterile, morally bankrupt, alarmingly humourless, intellectually barren, self-important, bullying, bombastic, inflexible, mendacious, cynical, self-serving, racist, boorish and ignorant, a preposterous preening popinjay constantly craving adoration.

And he holds the highest political office on the planet.

All the above might just be bearable were the world not facing the biggest threat of our lifetimes, a threat that without co-operation and leadership of those we vote into power, could see us as a species vanish from the face of the planet.

Where are our visionaries, our inspiring examples, our great men and women to stir us into a positive and empathetic resilience, not merely to division?

Trump once forecast, with his normal visionary hubris 'The China virus will just go away.' Yet even now it mutates to various forms, always ahead of the game. It outwits us, lying low before rising again with a vengeance.
And it makes mincemeat of Donald Trump.
Help.

 WEDNESDAY SEPT 2

WHO COULD EVER IMAGINE TOM FORREST AND PRUE HAVING SEX?

The Archers limps its way back to some kind of normality after several weeks of pandemic-enforced monologues, which attempt to delve the inner thoughts of the characters. It's soon obvious they don't have any. Listeners naturally switched off in their thousands and found something more stimulating to do, such as striking matches and then blowing them out.
The only monologue for the omnibus edition (where did that omnibus travel from and to? pondered young Mortimer) was Tom Forrest's introduction. Tom, the gamekeeper, would offer cosy thoughts on some aspect of rural life, after which, for those of us still awake, we listened to the past week's episodes.
I could never imagine ruddy-cheeked Tom (for thus I saw him) and his cosy wife Prue having sex, but that applied to almost every character in the series.
I spend a fair amount of time imagining different people having sex, so this probably explained my non-devotion to *The Archers*, despite a lukewarm interest. It's often a serial of clunky dialogue which seems to fill some vital national need.
Meantime, there's an enquiry as to what happened to the long bike rides undertaken weekly at the pandemic's onset by myself, The Fidler (aka Alan Fidler) and Tommy McClements (aka The Irish Rake). The rides persist. We three are somewhere between *The Last of the Summer Wine* trio (a certain maturity of age), *The Goodies* (who also rode bikes) or *The Three Stooges* (work it out for yourself).
Every Thursday finds us cycling 12–15 leisurely miles through

North Tyneside's marvellously arboreal waggonways network. Occasionally we tackle 30 plus miles, when Northumberland's hills remind us that our Tour de France days have passed.
Even on hot days, the Irish Rake arrives wearing clothes more suited to Scott of the Antarctic, thick long socks and a heavy tracksuit. The Fidler, enigmatic as ever, meets us with a wordless nod of the head, then cycles off to take up navigator position. Off we go. Many of our journeys' pleasures remain unspoken. But then we are of course, men.

PLANET *Corona* SATURDAY SEPT 5

THE STRANGE RITUAL OF OUR ARCHAIC COMMUNAL SONGS

With the pandemic still on the loose, there's much fuss around the Proms and the singing (or not) of our two tub-thumping slices of patriotism, *Land of Hope & Glory* and *Rule Britannia*. Do we risk, in our lusty bellowing, inadvertently spitting the deadly germ over fellow audience members, or is this merely the smokescreen tactic of those seeing the whole thing as dangerous nonsense anyway?

It's hard to deny that many of the two songs' words come over as jingoistic tosh.

They also use a linguistic currency that no-one now speaks – well, maybe the Amish religious movement, but few others. The verses are liberally sprinkled with 'thee', 'thy', 'thou' and 'thine', not to mention the occasional 'e'er' and 'o'er'. The tone's a bit dodgy too, with such lines as *'When Britain first, at Heaven's command/Arose from out the azure main'* which makes it sound suspiciously like we are God's chosen people – and we all know where that kind of thinking can lead.

There's a similar ambition for divine preference in the *Land of Hope and Glory* line, *God who made thee mighty, make thee mightier yet*. This is then repeated in case God didn't hear the first time and also to let our enemies know we've got a direct line to heaven for reinforcements.

Some years ago, along with other writers, I was commissioned to rewrite the words to several hymns in a more modern currency. I enjoyed this; it felt like taking a vigorous broom to a very dusty cupboard and, I hope, did not destroy the importance of the sentiments.

Will future generations look back on this strange Proms finale with wry amusement and think, did we REALLY sing that?? Or maybe no-one much listens to the words anyway. Here's an idea. Keep those stirring tunes, but prior to next year, run a competition for new, more relevant lyrics, words to inspire us but in less sabre-rattling, breast-beating, archaic fashion. I'd be up for that. And these days we all need to sing.

PLANET Corona   WEDNESDAY SEPT 9

HOLIDAYS? TRY A TRIP UP THE ROAD!

As we battle this beastly bug to our best, as we valiantly vie with this venomous virus (I've warned you about that alliterative excess before – Ed) I am minded to think about home. Home, as in do we now prefer to work from home rather than battle the daily commute? Home, as in do we now eschew the misery of holiday flights and quarantine and indulge the century's ugliest word, 'staycation'?

(A joke: 'My boss won't let me work from home.'
'What's your job?'
'I'm a deep sea diver'.
Second joke: 'I'm homesick'.
'But you are home.'
'Yes and I'm sick of it'.)

Millions of us cramming into trains, buses and cars at the identical time to battle our congested way to jobs we may well hate anyway, then battling back in the same miserable conditions later may eventually come to be seen with the same incredulity we now reserve for the Victorians sending young boys up chimneys.

Having been lucky enough to spend most of my working life outside real jobs – I have been a freelance author since the 1980s – my usual daily commute is across several feet of carpet.

This brings a certain freedom but also makes me easy prey to a succession of rough looking lads on the doorstep with a suitcase full of overpriced window wipes, none of whom (the lads) can I send away empty-handed.

I confess to missing the banter, the sociability and the gossip of life in an office, but all that may have gone now anyway.

As for holidays; there must be some advantages to waiting six hours then being asked to remove belt, shoes, rings and necklaces in order to board a delayed flight which proves to be full of drunken, raucously bellowing laddos, where you're sat next to a sweaty 18-stoner well endowed with halitosis.

I'll eventually think of them.

Meantime, try for once taking a brief holiday where you live. My partner Kitty and I once booked into The Grand Hotel Tynemouth (a mile away) and saw all things familiar in a new light.

Happy travelling!

SATURDAY SEPT 12

THE LEADING GOVERNMENT MINISTER HIDING IN THE DUSTBIN

Our intrepid reporter, looking for clarifications on recent confusions, tracked down a leading government minister.

He was hiding in a dustbin. The minister, not our reporter.

REP There you are minister. Perhaps you could explain the current rules on who can meet up with who else, where, when, for how long?

MIN Well, I think the rules are fairly straightforward and have been for at least the last three minutes.

REP So perhaps you could explain them?

MIN Well, as far as I can see, the answers are (a) not too many, (b) not too often, (c) not too long.

REP There seems some confusion on just who should get tested for the virus

MIN Ah, that's easy! If you've got no symptoms, don't get a test!

REP But surely we now know that many thousands of younger people are likely to be carriers without any symptoms. Yet they are still liable to infect others. What do you think about them?

MIN I think our young people are world beaters. The National Health Service too.

REP Some people are getting angry about those who flout the rules. Do you feel comfortable about people breaking the law?

MIN We'll have no truck with rule breakers, saboteurs, anarchists, tree huggers and people who chant in the street or provocatively wear woolly hats.

REP I was thinking of the Prime Minister breaking the EU withdrawal agreement. Or again, Dominic Cummings.

MIN Sssssh! His Venerable One might hear. (UNDER HIS BREATH) Mind, I do wish he would iron his tops.

REP Basically, does the government break the law whenever it wants, but expect us to pay a whopping fine for say, forgetting a mask?

MIN I'm glad you mentioned masks. We have six thousand now – or is it twenty eight trillion? – and I'm even confident some of them work. I know someone who wore a mask for six days and never got the virus. That makes you proud to be British. (PAUSE). You ARE British, I assume? Not an illegal immigrant? If so, you have to go back. That's the law. Plain and simple. Goodbye.
(EXIT REPORTER)

THURSDAY SEPT 17

THE FABLE OF SMITH AND THE MENACE OF THOSE HEDGE CLIPPERS

Fable for today: Smith was keeping open an option to break the law. It probably wouldn't happen and it if it did, it wouldn't be his fault. His close neighbour these past forty-odd years was acting suspiciously and aggressively.

Smith thought the neighbour might do something nasty. Smith thought the neighbour might do him in. The way he brandished those hedge-clippers in his garden the last week. The way he'd whistled once in the street.

And he'd banged on Smith's front door more than once at 4am. Smith said this was deliberately confrontational. Each time he'd asked Smith if he could keep the music down, Smith had told him where to get off. Smith had told told him he wanted nothing more to do with him or his greasy mates, then slammed the door in his face. So now Smith had worked out this plan, hunched up in his blanket.

Even the slightest hint from now on that the neighbour might do him in – even a glimpse of the hedge-clippers say – and Smith would do HIM in first. He knew it would be breaking the law but he told himself it was fully justified and it would be the neighbour's fault, not Smith's. Things were never Smith's fault. End of fable ...

Meanwhile, the Premier League returns – odd in more ways than one. Newcastle United win their opening game – AND away from home AND with no goals against.

Last season became a sad affair, drained of real passion; months of no games, followed by hollow, spectator-free contests. But now it's born anew! Except it's not. Everything is exactly the same. A nightmare?

For a sizeable group of people, that's a laughable thought. For those who do not understand football frenzy (and there are a lot), those who do not anguish over the chances of Andy Carroll ever scoring again, the recent close season has been a welcome absence of twenty-two rather dull men kicking a ball about and more dull men in studios mouthing platitudes and clichés about it. This group, who seem to lead happy enough lives, don't get it. *(published in error one day late!)*

PLANET Corona
SATURDAY SEPT 19

WHAT? THE ONE HUNDREDTH PLANET CORONA COLUMN?!

INT	It seems, Mortimer that you have been pestering us to interview you for a special occasion?
MORT	How indebted I would be for the privilege.
INT	Might I enquire as to what that occasion is?
MORT	A milestone, a landmark, a veritable historic moment.
INT	What is it?
MORT	The one hundredth Planet Corona column.
INT	Oh, I see.
MORT	I thought perhaps some small celebration?
INT	What had you in mind, exactly?
MORT	Oh, nothing too grand, you understand ...
INT	Well, go on.
MORT	Maybe we could stage a large firework display over the Tyne?
INT	Hmm.
MORT	And possibly a twenty-one gun salute fired off by Alan Shearer?
INT	Ah ...
MORT	Nothing ostentatious ... I assume there would be a tribute from the Queen, from the Buckingham Palace balcony?
INT	Well–
MORT	And I take it the Red Arrows would stage one of their spectacular aerial shows the length and breadth of the country?
INT	Ye-es. We'll keep it under review. I could maybe ask you a few short questions.
MORT	Take as many weeks as you like.

INT	I understand this column was originally written on a daily basis?
MORT	For seventy-five columns, every day, apart from Sunday.
INT	So what happened to that quotidian output?
MORT	It all got to me, you see. I found myself putting brown sauce on my Weetabix …Then I fell down in a heap, twitching badly.
INT	Since when it has been twice weekly?
MORT	And the spots have receded considerably.
INT	In this troubled and confused time, do the words of these one hundred columns offer any comfort?
MORT	A tramp in a Gateshead cemetery claimed my column gave the best insulation of any newspaper.
INT	Is Covid 19 not too serious a subject matter to be treated with humour, satire, even absurdity?
MORT	You have a way with words.
INT	And the future?
MORT	When Capt.Tom got to a hundred, there was a knighthood in it for him.
INT	Surely you're not suggesting–
MORT	I'm free next week, that's all I'm saying.
INT	Thank you, Mortimer.
MORT	No, thank you.

END

Five Bonus Tracks*

Donated at no extra charge

PLANET

SATURDAY SEPT 26

LET PROSE GIVE WAY TO POETRY – IF ONLY FOR ONE DAY..........

And for today's offering, dear readers, I offer you a poetic response to a very unpoetic virus.

CORONA BLUES
We never liked pneumonia
Mumps was not much fun
Scarlet fever left us ratty
After shingles we felt glum
Not a single vote for smallpox
Lukewarm on Asian flu
Ebola got no house room
From the likes of me and you

But here's a brand new ball game
Here's a beast that's run amok
Here comes a monster from a micro
Oh, the trauma! Oh, the shock!

Corona blues, corona blues
They can send us all mad, they can drive us to booze
It's the most awful thing that we've never seen
That teeny, all-powerful, Covid-19
Heads we don't win. Tails we still lose
They won't go away, those Corona blues

It's national, it's global,
it gets everywhere
It travels on wings
It dances on air
It speaks Spanish, it speaks French
English, Russian and Greek
It lays low mighty monarchs
The bold and the meek

It brings to their knees
Asians, Afghans and Poles
It laughs at our passports
And our border controls
More than eight million species
Inhabit this place
But it picks just the one
Our own human race

Corona blues, corona blues
They can send us all mad, they can drive us to booze
It's the most awful thing that we've never seen
That teeny, all-powerful. Covid-19
Heads we don't win. Tails we still lose
They won't go away, those Corona blues

PLANET Corona WEDNESDAY SEPT 30

WHY THE DOCTOR STOOD ON HIS HEAD IN THE WHEELIE BIN

(A PATIENT IS TALKING TO THE DOCTOR ONLINE)

PAT Everything just seems to be getting worse, Doc
DOC Really?
PAT I'm totally confused. No-one can go anywhere, do anything, meet anyone. Are we expected to sit in a room and stare at the cat?
DOC You're lucky to have a cat. So, these new restrictions are having side-effects then?
PAT I'm bewildered. I keep vomiting all the time, I fall asleep fifteen times a day, I get back ache, I have double vision, I keep shouting out 'Cardboard!' for no reason, I have lost my right nipple – and I regularly miss the 48 bus
DOC Zzzzzzz......
PAT You've fallen asleep, Doc!
DOC Sorry. It keeps happening these days. And the stress of this pandemic is sending me loopy. Sometimes I think I can't take any more

PAT You too, eh, doc?
DOC I bit my wife this morning, then I put the Coco-Pops in the spin drier and stood on my head in the wheelie bin.
PAT I often stand in the corner of the room and scream.
DOC Does your wife say anything?
PAT She's screaming in the opposite corner.
DOC Some people find gardening good therapy. Converse with the gladioli, that kind of thing and -
PAT Zzzzzzz.....
DOC Now YOU'VE fallen asleep!
PAT Sorry. It keeps happening these days.
DOC Anyway – gardening?
PAT I did try mowing the front lawn.
DOC Any good?
PAT Not really. I'd forgotten we paved it over last year. Has anyone got the remotest idea of how we should be handling all this lot?
DOC Have you tried senna pods?
PAT No
DOC Me neither.
PAT Is there any hope for the planet, Doc?
DOC We could get hit by a giant asteroid. Bang! That would put us out of our misery.
PAT They said this would be all over by Christmas.
DOC They said that about the Ice Age.
PAT Is coronavirus just toying with us, Doc? Maybe the human race's time is up?
DOC Well, your time is up anyway. Thank you (CLICKS ONTO NEXT PATIENT)

SATURDAY OCT 17

TIME TO GIVE TURKEY THE BIRD

There's a Christmas turkey crisis – it's the fault of coronavirus. Many people are eschewing their usual juggernaut sized bird because (a) they're out of work – the people not the turkeys – or (b) restrictions make the normal family sized gathering impossible. Turkey breeders are weeping and wailing and crying 'woe is me!' Yet there's much to applaud in both these downsizings. Most big Christmas family get-togethers end up with one of the following; simmering unspoken tensions, outbreaks of tears, loud arguments, or a sudden punch-up between the surly cousin and that drunken uncle who just vomited over the baby.

To return to the turkey. We eat it instinctively at Christmas (vegetarians and vegans will excuse me these musings) even though few of us like it. It's as dry as cardboard and inordinately dull compared to beef, lamb or pork. To compound the masochism, we insist on the unspeakable horrors of bread sauce as an accompaniment.

If we do like turkey, why do we not eat it on the other 364 days of the year? Or make that 358 days, as we spend the week after Christmas Day eating our glum way through the remnants of the wretched bird via curries, sandwiches, soups and salads.

Onto the radicalisation of Metro mayors, a process hastened by the pandemic. The old-style mayors were uncontroversial figures sporting heavy golden chains over their shoulders.

Their functions included opening new libraries, planting the first tree on the new housing development or handing over a cheque to a worthy charity. They were chauffeured round in a big black car by a man in a peaked hat.

No-one took the old style mayors that seriously. The new breed of political northern Metro Mayors, (plus the London Mayor Sadiq Khan) are much more gobby, feisty, controversial and now openly challenging the national government under the inspiration of our modern Wat Tyler, Manchester's Andy Burnham. They seem to be tempered with a steel missing from most politicians. North of the Tyne's Jamie Driscoll is also flexing his muscles.

Exciting signs in an horrendous time – as if the common voice of the people were swelling up via these Metro Mayors, and its message is, *Whatever else, we shall not live overlong like caged animals.*

SATURDAY OCTOBER 24

DICK TURPIN, THE LONE RANGER AND THE MYSTERIOUS WOMEN OF YEMEN

Consider the changing culture of masks. Masks were once worn by such unlikely bedfellows as bank robbers and surgeons and occasionally by the privileged dilettantes attending the annual masked ball at the local stately home.

These last facial appendages though were often eye masks, usually more ornamental than functional and not fooling anyone. However, somehow both the Lone Ranger and Dick Turpin managed to carry it off, in Turpin's case often along with the female coach travellers' jewels.

Donald Trump (as usual) got it all wrong when recently mentioning the Lone Ranger's mask in relation to his own Covid-19 mask antics, or mainly non-antics.

Though I confess I do like Trump in a proper face mask. It disguises that anus mouth. Having a mouth so like an anus seems strangely symbolic for Donald Trump. I could elaborate but good taste prevents me from so doing.

I grew accustomed to masked faces some years back when trekking three weeks through the wilds of Yemen, researching a play. Yemen is the poorest and most traditional Arabic country (also the most generous to strangers). You would as likely see an unmasked Yemeni woman in public as you would see one unclothed. The only part of the female Yemeni body exposed in public is the eyes. This gives the eyes a strange allure and sense of mystery and also influences our interaction. For where else can we look?

In normal non-mask social interactions our gaze is drawn to the other person's mouth as they talk. You could of course stare at the wart on their ear but I'm sure your social graces would not allow it, at least more than briefly. Only when the other person is more of an intimate, or when perhaps both parties harbour a desire for there to be some intimacy, do we tend to indulge more than occasional eye contact. That's the case in buttoned-up UK, anyway. But where now, with face masks becoming more ubiquitous? Strangely enough I still find myself staring at the area of mask that hides the mouth itself; curious to see the material puff in and out with each breath. Yes, I do realise I am talking to a piece of cloth. Yet one more strange activity on the increasingly strange Planet Corona.

PLANET *Corona* — SATURDAY OCT 31

THE YEAR THAT SANTA MAY MAKE HIS GREAT ESCAPE

A knock at the front door revealed Father Christmas.
'Two metres please,' I said, motioning him back.
'What, but–'
'Rub this hand gel on' I said, pointing to the container.
'Yes, OK but–'
'Put this mask on' I said.
He had a bit of trouble getting it round his copious beard. To tell the truth he looked a bit ridiculous, but just about managed.
'What do you want?' I asked.
'I'm confused,' he said.
'We're all confused' I said. 'I'm confused. My neighbours are confused. The lollipop lady is confused. The prime minister is confused. Sometimes I think even my goldfish is confused'.
'You have a goldfish?'
'No, it's a joke', I said. 'The only person who doesn't seem confused right now is sitting in the White House'.
'What?'
'The orange maniac. But then the insane often seem to have a deluded lucidity. Anyway, what's your gripe, Claus?'
'What the hell's happening with Christmas?' he asked. 'Is it cancelled?'
'Who knows?' I said.
'I need to know' he said. 'That's why I've come ahead on this rekky. I need to plan my timeline, my production schedule, my labour force'.
'Labour force?'
'Two thousand Elves'.

'How did you get here?' I asked.
'I rode bareback on Dancer,' he said. 'Now I've got a really sore arse.'
Suddenly I realised a large reindeer was eating my tiny flower patch.
'Where's the sleigh?' I asked.
'Being serviced.'
'You might need to isolate for fourteen days'. I said. 'What's your bubble?'
'Bubble?'
'Never mind. You look frozen.'
'You'd be bloody frozen as well, on the back of that reindeer.'
'Look' I said, 'I shouldn't really do this but you can come in, sit the far end of the room. I'll give you a cup of tea.'
'I usually get a glass of sherry and a mince pie.' he said.
'Don't push it, Claus' I said.
'So is Christmas happening this year or not?' he asked.
'Sort of. Call it a Corona Christmas.'
'And what about me?'
'Going into fifteen million different houses? Some in Tier Three? Forget it. Stay home. Watch *The Great Escape*.'
'Phew! That's a relief! A year off from all this lot.'
And with one bound, Santa and Dancer were gone.

"*That's all Folks!*"

Other books by Peter Mortimer

Documentary/Travel
The Last of the Hunters (Five Leaves)
Broke Through Britain (Mainstream)
100 Days on Holy Island (Mainstream)
Cool For Qat (Mainstream)
Camp Shatila (Five Leaves)
Made in Nottingham (Five Leaves)
The Chess Traveller (Red Squirrel)

Poetry
A Rainbow in its Throat (Flambard)
I Married the Angel of the North (Five Leaves)
Utter Nonsense (IRON Press)

Fable
The Witch and the Maiden (Pivot Press)
Croak, The King & a Change in the Weather (Flambard/IRON)

Plays
Riot (Five Leaves)
Off the Wall (Five Leaves)
Playtime (Flambard)
Death at Dawn (Red Squirrel)
Victor Noble Rainbird (IRON Press)

Novella
Uninvited (Red Squirrel)

Newspaper Columns
Mortimer at Large (IRON/NorthTyneside Libraries)

IRON Press is among the country's longest established independent literary publishers. The press began operations in 1973 with IRON Magazine which ran for 83 editions until 1997. Since 1975 we have also brought out a regular list of individual collections of poetry, fiction and drama plus various anthologies ranging from *Voices of Conscience, Limerick Nation, The Poetry of Perestroika, 100 Island Poems* and *Cold Iron, Ghost Stories from the 21st Century* and *The IRON Book of Tree Poetry* and forthcoming, *Aliens* (fiction).

The press is one of the leading independent publishers of haiku in the UK.
Since 2013 we have also run a biennial IRON Press Festival round the harbour in our native Cullercoats. The IRON OR Festival took place in June 2019.

We are delighted to be a part of Inpress Ltd, which was set up by Arts Council England to support independent literary publishers.
Go to our website (www.ironpress.co.uk) for full details of our titles and activities.